WORLD RELIGIONS AND WORLD PEACE
The International Inter-Religious Symposium on Peace

WORLD RELIGIONS AND WORLD PEACE
✍ ✍ ✍ ✍ THE INTERNATIONAL INTER-
RELIGIOUS SYMPOSIUM ON PEACE ✍ ✍
EDITED BY HOMER A. JACK ✍ ✍ ✍ ✍ ✍
PREFACE BY PRESIDENT ZAKIR HUSAIN
INTRODUCTION BY
DANA McLEAN GREELEY

BEACON PRESS : BOSTON

CONTENTS

Preface, by President Zakir Husain   vii
Introduction, by Dana McLean Greeley   xi
1. The Symposium Message   1
2. The Symposium Papers: Common Religious Concerns   4
   Panel 1. Social and Economic Development   5
   Panel 2. Freedom and Human Rights   8
   Panel 3. Peace-Making and Peace-Keeping   9
3. Inaugural Papers   16
   Shri R. R. Diwakar, M.P.   16
   Shri Jayaprakash Narayan   21
   Bishop John Wesley Lord   27
   Shri G. Ramachandran, M.P.   32
   Homer A. Jack   35
4. Sanctions for Peace (I)   39
   Hinduism, by Swami Ranganathananda   39
   Islam, by K. G. Saiyadain   49
   Zoroastrianism, by Dastoor N. D. Minochehr-
      Homji   57
   Judaism, by Rabbi Maurice N. Eisendrath   61
   Sikhism, by Gopal Singh, M.P.   75
5. Sanctions for Peace (II)   84
   Vira Shaivism: Hinduism, by Jagadguru Shri
      Gangadhar Rajayogeendra Mahaswamiji
      Moorusavirmath, Hubli   84

Christianity, by Rt. Rev. John H. Burt   100
Buddhism, by Ven. Baddeeama Wimalawansa
    Thero   109
Jainism, by Bool Chand   114
6. The Relevance of Gandhi as a Religious Force for
    Peace, by Shri G. Ramachandran, M.P.   124
7. The Role of Religion in Building World Peace   130
Ralph David Abernathy   130
Archbishop Angelo Fernandes   137
Msgr. Edward G. Murray   143
Rev. Riri Nakayama   148
Jambel D. Gomboev   153
Shri U. N. Dhebar   155
8. A World Conference on Religion and Peace,
    by Homer A. Jack   160
Symposium Conclusions   169
9. Closing Session   171
Hon. Morarji Desai   171
Hon. Harold E. Stassen   176
Karan Singh   179

Appendix A   184
1. Rev. G. Nichidatsu Fujii   184
2. The Japanese-American Inter-Religious Consulta-
    tion on Peace   188
3. The Interim Advisory Committee for a World
    Conference on Religion and Peace   192
4. Symposium Participants   195

Appendix B   201
The World Conference for International Peace
    Through Religion   201

Appendix C   207
Contributors to This Volume   207

President Zakir Husain

LET IT BE CLEAR in our minds that in spite of all advances in science and technology, religions still exercise a powerful influence on the minds of millions of human beings. The majority of the people of the world belong to one religion or another. Great issues continue to be settled, consciously or unconsciously, against the background of religious convictions. It will be unwise for anyone to ignore religious influences in finding solutions for world problems, big or small.

Let us also understand that all religions teach the reality of God and obedience to the will of God which translate as goodwill and peace among men. All religions have their systems of ethics. Religions and ethics have marched hand in hand throughout history. This perhaps is the reason religions continue to be of great significance in lifting man above the animal kingdom. Religions have helped considerably to humanize human relations and to create and sustain the higher values of human conduct. Although hatred, violence, and evil have persisted in the world, it is a matter for conjecture what the situation might have been without religious influences. We are often apt to forget the might-have-beens!

However, let us not forget that religious passions have sometimes become accessory to conflicts and wars. During their long history, religions became confined within circles of their own and competitions and conflicts developed among them. Perhaps these competitions and conflicts have led to deeper introspection of the human soul with the ultimate result that truth, love, and nonviolence have received a fuller confirmation. One of the heartening trends in our time is the increasing inter-religious cooperation and harmony which we now witness in different parts of the world. The winds of liberalization blowing within the Roman Catholic church and the consequent rapprochement between it and the rest of the Christian world is undoubtedly one of these significant trends. Buddhism and Hinduism have also come closer to each other in recent times. We have also witnessed uplifting influences sweeping through Islam. All these changes have inevitably led to the reassertion of higher spiritual, ethical, and cultural values. They will help us to move, however slowly, towards a more united human community in good time.

The supreme challenge of the century in which we live, arising from advances in both science and religion, is to move towards the one-world community. Just as we now have great national federations like the U.S.A., the U.S.S.R., and India, so we must not hesitate to think in terms of a world federation, world law, a world court, and a world police force preserving the autonomy of nations and at the same time preventing wars and violent conflicts among them. This will, of course, mean disarmament, which may progress slowly, but nations must disarm nevertheless. The religions of the world, which all teach and emphasize the supremacy of God and the law of goodwill and peace among men, will have to play a fuller and more conscious part in the future than they have in the past in leading man to such a goal. Religions can and, therefore, must influence the mind of man positively to achieve the great goal of the one-world community.

But in order that religions may effectively play this historic role, they will have to look beyond dogmas, rituals, and practices which obstruct the flow of life from different religious circles towards a new sense of harmony and collaboration. This will mean nothing less than the self-purification of every religious community from within. Who can deny that all religious communities need today to undergo such self-purification? Once this is achieved it will be found that the path to harmony and cooperation among religions lies open without any obstruction.

Mahatma Gandhi, in our own lifetime, equated spirituality to truth, and ethics to nonviolence. To him the core of every religion was truth and nonviolence, with love linking the two. From this belief flowed his teaching of unreserved reverence for all the great religions in the world. Reverence is more than tolerance. Gandhi asked for much more than tolerance among the great religious systems. He pleaded for deep mutual understanding and the humility to learn from each other.

We must also take care not to pit science and religion against each other, however contradictory they might appear on the surface. On the contrary, we must put them together for the good of man. Science without religion becomes rudderless in terms of human destiny, and religion without science tends to superstition and reaction. The gap between religion and science, if not closed, will be fatal to the growth and progress of human society.

World peace today depends largely upon the marriage of religion and science. Religion should point to the direction of peace and science should find the means by which human society can move towards a united, prosperous, happy, and peaceful world community.

The purpose of this Symposium, as is evident, is for the representatives of different religions to recover the profound heritage of truth, love, and nonviolence in every religion and then to resolve firmly that this heritage not be allowed to remain dormant. It must be recovered because it can be re-covered. It has now to be reapplied to the solution of the great problem of achieving world peace.

We have now long realized that peace and justice are indivisible. Peace without justice will be short-lived, and justice without peace will be a contradiction. Religious leadership must reckon with this interdependence of peace and justice. Who can understand the indivisibility of the two more than true votaries of the great religions which keep the love of God and the love of man in their hearts? If religious leaders will stand for peace and justice unequivocally, then we take a big step towards world peace. We want peace between individuals and groups within nations and peace among the nations. These are all vitally interdependent. If the spirit of the Sermon on the Mount, Buddha's philosophy of compassion, the Hindu concept of *ahiṁsā*, and the passion of Islam for obedience to the will of God can combine, then we shall see generated the most potent influence for world peace.

Let each one of us return from this International Inter-Religious Symposium to his or her religious constituency with the determination that the message of this Symposium will be the watchword of all our work hereafter. Then something significant can happen to strengthen the forces of peace in the world. The world is on the brink of great peril, perhaps the suicide of the race in a nuclear war. We must push back this peril with all the strength in us, and we can best do so as men and women of deep religious and ethical convictions which have the sanction of centuries and which have never been proved to be without deep significance in building a just and peaceful human society.

INTRODUCTION

Dana McLean Greeley

AT THE National Inter-Religious Conference on Peace, held
in Washington in March 1966, the almost 500 participants
voted to "explore the possibilities for calling a World Inter-
Religious Conference on Peace in 1967, encompassing participation of all the world's religious traditions."[1] The U.S.
Inter-Religious Committee on Peace, which grew out of this
national conference (there had been a previous American
committee and smaller gatherings since 1962), sent an exploratory mission to North Africa and Asia to sound out the
possibilities of a world conference. Rev. Herschel Halbert of
the Department of Christian Social Relations of the Executive
Council of the Episcopal church and Dr. Homer A. Jack of
the Department of Social Responsibility of the Unitarian
Universalist Association of North America spent several
months in the spring of 1967 discussing the problem especially
with African and Asian religious leaders. In April 1967,
the conclusions were reported to the U.S. Committee.[2] They
can be summarized as follows:

There have been no successful attempts, since 1945 at
least, to bring together the leaders of the major world
religions to discuss substantively the problems of world peace.
The need to convene such a world inter-religious conference
was widely felt, and the time appeared ripe to do so. The tasks

[1] The proceedings of this conference are available in *Religion and Peace:
Papers from the National Inter-Religious Conference on Peace*, edited by
Homer A. Jack. Indianapolis: Bobbs-Merrill. 137 pp. 1966.
[2] The full report is available as *From Geneva/Rome Through Tokyo*, by
Herschel Halbert and Homer A. Jack. Boston and New York: U.S. Inter-
Religious Committee on Peace. 43 pp. 1967.

of organizing such a world conference are formidable. They involve at least the following problems: 1. Bringing the leaders of world religions to the same stage of readiness to talk substantively about issues of world peace. 2. Finding a site which would be politically and religiously neutral. 3. Securing balanced initial sponsorship so that the conference would not be dominated either by United States religious leaders or Judeo-Christian leaders. 4. Obtaining funds to pay the international travel costs of many if not most of the delegates.

The exploratory mission concluded that a preparatory symposium would be necessary to plan the larger world conference. Even the calling of a preparatory symposium appeared difficult. This involved careful planning over a six-month period. It necessitated the sponsorship by at least one non-American organization or institution in addition to the U.S. Committee. It demanded prior commitment for attendance by a sufficient number of United States religious leaders. A symposium necessitated the help of two staff members from the U.S. Committee. Finally, the symposium had to have adequate subsidy and this had to come principally from religious sources in the United States. The exploratory mission then made this final recommendation: That an exploratory symposium be held in 1968, preferably in New Delhi, with possibly the Gandhi Peace Foundation as a cosponsor, or in Tokyo, with an *ad hoc* inter-religious committee as a cosponsor. The U.S. Committee meeting in April 1967 considered these recommendations and reached a somewhat different decision. It voted to explore further the convening of two, two-nation, inter-religious consultations, one Japanese-American in Tokyo and the other Indian-American in New Delhi. It was further agreed that these two consultations or symposia would be the right next steps preliminary to a possible world conference.

Further explorations were made with both individuals and groups in Tokyo and New Delhi. Interest appeared in the form of the International Seminars Subcommittee of the National Committee for the Gandhi Centenary in India. Dr. Homer A. Jack visited India again in September 1967, and at that time Shri G. Ramachandran, chairman of the seminars subcommittee, agreed to the convening of an International Inter-Religious Symposium on Peace in New Delhi in mid-January. It would be cosponsored by the International Seminars Subcommittee and the U.S. Committee, with Shri Ramachandran and Dr. Jack as joint secretaries. This proved later to be a most fortunate and effective combination.

The finances of such an international gathering are always a problem, especially with the unavailability of foreign exchange in some nations. The Gandhi Centenary Committee agreed to pay all costs of the Symposium inside India, including the room and board of participants. The U.S. Committee agreed to pay other costs, including one-half the travel costs of non-Indian, non-American delegates. This was made possible by generous contributions from a number of participating American denominations and a grant from the Johnson Foundation of Racine, Wisconsin. The total budget of the Symposium amounted to 27,300 rupees ($39,000), not including the exploratory mission which was underwritten completely by the U.S. Committee. These costs also do not include staff time which was contributed to this ecumenical undertaking by the several organizations involved, especially the Episcopal church, the Unitarian Universalist Association, and the Gandhi Peace Foundation.

Preparations for the Symposium centered in the offices of the Gandhi Peace Foundation in New Delhi. Dr. Jack joined the staff in December as participants were recruited from around the world.

In the United States in the meantime, the U.S. Committee recruited an ecumenical team to make a round-the-world consultation on peace, the central stop of which was to be the Symposium in New Delhi. Under the capable executive lead-

ership of Rev. Herschel Halbert, and later with help from
Herman Will, Jr., a representative team was assembled which
included the following persons: Dr. Ralph D. Abernathy,
Le Roy Anderson, Most Rev. Joseph L. Bernardin, Dr.
Desmond W. Bittinger, Rt. Rev. John Harris Burt, Rabbi
Maurice N. Eisendrath, Dr. Dana McLean Greeley, Dr.
Dorothy Hutchinson, Bishop John Wesley Lord, Bishop
James K. Mathews, Rev. Telford Mook, Msgr. Edward G.
Murray, and Gov. Harold E. Stassen. Rabbi Eisendrath, Dr.
Greeley, and Bishop Lord served as cochairmen of the team,
as they are three of the six cochairmen of the U.S. Committee.

Leaving New York on January 3, 1968, the team made official stops at the offices of the World Council of Churches in
Geneva, the Vatican in Rome, the Ecumenical Patriarchate
in Istanbul, and also in Jerusalem. While the main objective
was the Symposium in New Delhi, the members visited
Saigon for four days and then participated in a highly successful and significant Japanese-American Inter-Religious Consultation on Peace in Kyoto, where the findings and resolves
of New Delhi were confirmed and extended, and other plans
initiated.[3]

Further staff members of the American team were Henry
Hampton and Theodore Schiller; and others who attended
included Mrs. Eisendrath, Mrs. Jack, Mrs. Lord, Mrs.
Mathews, and Miss Anne Mathews.

The International Inter-Religious Symposium was held in
New Delhi from January 10, through 14, 1968. This volume
constitutes a detailed, faithful report of its program and ac-
complishments.

A total of forty-six participants attended, as well as eight
observers and eight additional consultants or speakers. They
came from nine nations: Ceylon, France, India, Japan,
Malaysia, the Soviet Union, Thailand, the United Kingdom,

---

[3] This report is available as *Report of the World Trip*. New York: U.S.
Inter-Religious Committee on Peace. 1968.

and the United States. These participants represented nine world religions: Buddhism, Catholicism, Hinduism, Islam, Jainism, Judaism, Protestantism, Sikhism, and Zoroastrianism.

The hospitality shown by the Indian hosts was overwhelming. Participants were invited to the Rashtrapathi Bhawan for a reception generously given by President Zakir Husain. Also attending the gathering in this former palace of the viceroys, and receiving the groups most graciously, was Her Excellency Mrs. Indira Gandhi, Prime Minister of India. At the close of the Symposium, the hosts took participants and observers on a special bus to visit the Taj Mahal at Agra by daylight and moonlight.

A number of achievements for the Symposium can be modestly recorded.

Perhaps the greatest achievement was that the Symposium was held. Representatives from nine world religions met for five days to discuss substantive issues on world peace. Despite large and continuing differences in religion, nationality, and politics, there were common agreements of more than the most superficial kind. These included not only the Symposium Message but the three panel reports.

A second achievement was that dialogue occurred without the specter of syncretism. There was a genuine toleration of differences. No attempt was made to hide deep differences in theology and culture, and yet these differences did not prevent certain overriding agreements.

Still a third achievement was the agreement to proceed to organize a broader, larger world conference on religion and peace.

A fourth achievement was the presentation of a model for national inter-religious committees on peace. The creation of such national committees initially in India and Japan appears likely, in addition to that already in existence in the United States.

Another achievement was that the Symposium appeared helpful to the forces for peace within India. Not only was the widespread publicity in the Indian press valuable, but closer cooperation was forged between certain secular peace groups—such as the Gandhi Peace Foundation—and religious bodies.

A final achievement was that the Symposium illustrated or suggested for the American participants the continued usefulness of the U.S. Inter-Religious Committee on Peace on the world scene if it continues to work sensitively.

There were several inadequacies in the Symposium. The representation was not as wide religiously as had been anticipated. No Shintoists attended, nor were Moslems from outside India present.

The representation was not so wide geographically as had been anticipated. No Africans or Latin Americans were present. In truth, this introductory Symposium never was intended for complete, worldwide, balanced representation, but it was hoped until almost the last minute that there would be some representation from Africa and Latin America.

Neither was representation so wide politically as had been anticipated. Only three participants came from the communist world. We had hoped for others from the Soviet Union and eastern Europe if not, at this time, from the People's Republic of China, North Korea, or North Vietnam.

If more time could have been spent in preparation, and more travel funds earlier guaranteed, some but not all of the above deficiencies might have been lessened.

The Symposium for those present was a source of great inspiration and firm resolution, as well as of fond fellowship. There was a clear consensus that religious leaders must work together for peace, as a religious mandate and for the salvation of civilization. And they belong together, by their origin and to this end.

1. ✍ THE SYMPOSIUM MESSAGE

MOST INTERNATIONAL CONFERENCES try to summarize their thrust in a concise rhetorical statement. The International Symposium convened a small committee, headed by Shri R. R. Diwakar, to compose such a statement. This went through several drafts and was adopted unanimously at the final plenary session.

The participants and observers in this International Inter-Religious Symposium on Peace, meeting in New Delhi on January 10–14, 1968, having considered various aspects of peace and the role of religious institutions and men of religion in the establishment of lasting peace, issue this message to all men everywhere in our world:

Deeply concerned at the violent conflicts in today's world and the constant threat of their extension with greater destruction of life and property,

Filled with compassion for the sufferings and privations of the majority of mankind,

Dismayed at the ever-widening gap between affluent countries and needy regions and the social resentment and potential violence that go with it,

This International Inter-Religious Symposium on Peace calls upon all men to turn their thoughts to the securing of human rights, justice, and peace.

This Symposium solemnly affirms that international peace is an essential precondition and cornerstone of true human progress. Peace is indivisible and, when it does not exist in any single area, it cannot be said to exist fully anywhere else.

On the individual and national levels, pride and racial hatred, the spirit of selfishness, and the desire for power and prestige are at the root of all conflicts, together with the illusion that war and violence can solve human problems. Wars today create more problems than they solve. Man must now turn to peaceful ways. A new spirit must animate co-existence between individuals and peoples, and there must be a new outlook on man, his duties, and his destiny.

Committed as we are to the full acceptance of the brotherhood of man, we call upon all concerned with human values to give constant expression to the agonizing desire for peace. It is for all of us to arouse public opinion the world over in favor of peace with justice, with concern for the true welfare of all men, and to bring to bear on the minds and hearts of world leaders the intensity of this universal yearning for lasting peace.

Each man's inherent and fundamental right to be accepted with respect and reverence by all of his fellow men is basic to peace. We, therefore, appeal to all religious leaders to intensify their efforts to foster an ever greater understanding and respect for the beliefs of others. Religion must not be allowed to continue as a divisive force, but should be directed toward the furtherance of amity and brotherhood. Religious leaders should speak out courageously when the fundamental rights of man anywhere are endangered, particularly where minorities are involved.

Grave economic disparities, both within and between countries, threaten internal stability and progress, and give rise to tensions and conflict which imperil international peace. A converging one-world economy, functioning for the benefit not of one region only but of the entire human community, should be our constant goal.

This Symposium expresses the hope that far greater support will be given to existing international and national agencies committed to the cause of peace. Concerned leaders in all lands should work together for the establishment of stronger international machinery to serve the cause of peace with justice and freedom.

2. ⚚ THE SYMPOSIUM PAPERS: COMMON RELIGIOUS CONCERNS

PERHAPS THE MOST PRODUCTIVE PART of the Symposium consisted of the three simultaneous panels. Participants and observers were free to attend the panel of their choice. The first was on the topic, "Common Religious Concern for Social and Economic Development." It was chaired by Ven. Pimbure Soratha Thero, with Shri D. K. Gupta as *rapporteur* and Rev. A. J. Fonesca, S.J., as consultant. The second panel on "Common Religious Concern for Freedom and Human Rights" was chaired by Bishop W. Q. Lash, with Prof. M. Yamunacharya as *rapporteur* and Rev. Herschel Halbert as consultant. The third panel was on "Common Religious Concern for Peace-Making and Peace-Keeping." It was chaired by Gov. Harold E. Stassen, with Ven. Swami Bhaskaranandji as *rapporteur* and Dr. Dorothy Hutchinson as consultant. Each panel met three different times during the duration of the Symposium, and often there were additional meetings of officers and drafting committees.

The papers of the three panels were submitted to the final plenary session chaired by Dr. Dana McLean Greeley. The reports were received; there was not time for the full debate necessary for them to be formally approved, but their combined thrust certainly had the approval of most Symposium participants.

Panel 1. Social and Economic Development

PEACE IN THE WORLD is not possible while two-thirds of the human family suffers from hunger and deprivation. This disparity between the poor and the affluent in the economic and social state is a challenge to the highest teachings of the world religions that regard all men as brothers. Therefore the Symposium urges all religious groups to join together to express their deep concern for a full and harmonious development that will reach out to every individual and to all sections of mankind. In this way we may hope to narrow the ever widening gulf that exists between the privileged and less privileged. Neither religion nor prevailing economic or political programs and institutions have been able to motivate mankind to this urgent task. Yet until man expresses himself morally and spiritually through religion by sharing with those in greater need, the world which is becoming one technologically and materially will not feel nor act as one emotionally and mentally. The resulting tension will lead to violence and ultimately to annihilation.

The convergence of interests between developing and developed countries is becoming more evident as a result of the technological revolution. This fact should be faced squarely. Therefore the social and economic development of the world as one unit must be a common religious concern.

In order that religion may face the challenge of our technological era, this Symposium expresses the hope that every religion will take stock of the extent of its preparedness to meet the needs of a generation of men brought up in a technological environment and imbued with a scientific spirit of inquiry and reasoning. This will require serious consideration of their own religious concepts, values, and institutions by religious leaders. The goal of such a rethinking and readjustment should be to make their members personally and corporately realize the need to manifest their religious adherence by supporting the claims of social justice as between the privileged and the dispossessed and in creating a social consciousness to serve the common good both at the national and international level.

We believe that the religious community must assert the primary allegiance of man to man in the family of man and that human sovereignty precedes and transcends national sovereignty.

As an expression of our common religious compassion for human life where there is a clear and specific social or economic need, we urge that all religious groups in that area join together in order to discover how collectively that need can be met.

In the developing world, one of the most important factors retarding progress is the illiteracy of the masses and lack of educated and skilled personnel. Religious bodies could play a vital role in education among the people at all levels and inspire them to contribute to their own social and economic development. A similar role could be played by religious groups in stimulating self-help projects, in bringing about a better distribution of landed property and other material resources, and in motivating people's spirit for building a sound social order based on honesty, integrity, and mutual assistance.

Religious organizations and their members have a responsibility, not only to demonstrate through pioneering projects what can be done to meet human needs in specific situations, but also to influence national governments and leaders to use the resources at their disposal to advance the welfare and development of mankind throughout the world. The policies of the nations should reflect the interest of all mankind rather than a narrow conception of national interest. In addition, the United Nations and the regional organizations must be constantly reminded that they have a responsibility to serve more than their collective self-interest. They are called to serve humanity in its widest need.

With advancing technology and unchecked human avarice, the natural resources of the world—water, soil, and minerals as well as the animal and vegetable kingdoms—are being depleted at such a rate that the ecological balance of nature is threatened. These resources are entrusted to man to be used so that the generations to come may not be deprived of their rightful share in these gifts of God. Religious people with a long-range view should lead in calling for a halt to this march to destruction and for a sound program for conservation.

At the international level, the developed and the developing countries should make a special effort to evolve a global strategy so that there may be equitable development and distribution of the wealth of the world. For this purpose, the existing international organizations for granting economic and technical assistance to the developing countries should be strengthened and supported generously with a spirit of responsibility towards the entire world community. A concrete measure would include substantially larger proportions of aid in relation to the national product by developed countries, the lowering of their tariff barriers, and the creation of a world development fund out of the money formerly spent on armaments.

Another great concern for all religious people should be the manufacture of and trade in weapons of violence. The armament race not only threatens mankind with destruction, but it also means that millions will face death from starvation because the nations have chosen to use their resources for the production or purchase of weapons rather than food. The need for development capital is so great that the continuation

of present arms spending will doom two-thirds of the world
to a marginal existence for decades to come. The sale of
weapons to developing nations without regard to real security
needs imposes on them an unnecessary economic burden and
may lead to increased tension and regional conflict.

Thus an effective program for disarmament and international control over nuclear development is indispensable to
the building of a peaceful world.

Such spaces of earth like the oceans and the polar regions
which are not yet demarcated as belonging to any particular
nation-state should be brought under international control so
that the benefits derived from these natural resources may be
available to all the people of the world and properly utilized
for the welfare of coming generations.

Panel 2. Freedom and Human Rights

HUMAN RIGHTS should not be less than those declared by the
United Nations. All discrimination, based on caste or class,
creed or color, or national origin, must end. It was affirmed
that every individual in whatever part of the world he may be,
must have equality of opportunity to rise to the highest stature
of which he would be capable. The right of a man to continue to exist free from fear of extinction for the mere reason
that he belongs to this or that religious or other group must
be affirmed.

The religions of the world must speak with a unified voice
in upholding and defending these rights as they stem from
man's status and dignity as man.

Education should be utilized as an instrument for creating a
suitable moral climate, in all the several nations, in which to
achieve human rights, and the recognition of corresponding
duties and obligations.

International instruments, needed to guarantee human rights, should be brought into being in all the different nations.

Attempts should be made in each country and among the adherents of different religions to promote inter-religious mutual respect and understanding by opening channels of communication such as colloquia and dialogues in which the leaders of different religious groups would be brought together in a spirit of fellowship and common religious concern to achieve peace.

Attempts should be made by leaders and followers of different religions to bring their religious endeavors into close relation to social concerns, which include freedom and human rights, with a view to closing the gap between the so-called secular and the sacred. Religiously minded persons and institutions must make their own contributions and actively participate in programs, the objects of which are to combat hunger, poverty, disease, and ignorance.

Devotion to God should issue forth in acts of loving service, and the gulf between principle and performance among the religiously minded people has to be expeditiously and zealously bridged as a condition *sine qua non* of world peace achieved through religion.

As no problem in the present day is capable of being solved in isolation from the global context, a worldwide approach is called for among the religiously minded people of the world, and a dynamic recognition that we all belong to one another as members of a single family of humanity.

Panel 3. Peace-Making and Peace-Keeping

THE CONFEREES, representing a large number of different religions, considering together the subject of peace-making and peace-keeping, with prime attention to the moral considerations, agree in the following propositions: *

I. In this age, when upon this earth under God, scientific developments have expanded both the potential devastation of war and the creative productivity of peace, we hold:

A. There is an increasing moral conviction that war must be condemned as a means to settle disputes.

B. From a moral viewpoint, there is an urgent need for an increased restraint upon the violent use of military forces.

C. There is a moral obligation upon every human being, upon every organized group, and upon every nation to work affirmatively for peace with justice.

D. There is a moral principle that the entire human race should be encompassed universally within our constructive concern.

E. Morally the common well-being of all humanity should be given greater attention than the narrow sovereign self-interest of the nation-state.

F. The basic concept of creative freedom for all peoples establishes the moral principle that all should have the potential of a fair measure of fulfillment of life, of cultural participation, and of the pursuit of true individual happiness.

G. There is a moral need for integrity and trustworthiness in the conduct of public affairs, as well as in private matters in all states.

H. There is a moral responsibility upon each individual and each nation to make some helpful contribution to the lives of other human beings, especially to those less fortunate.

I. There is a moral requirement to try to prevent oppression and aggression and, when necessary, to restrain and defend against those who commit these and other crimes

---

* With the one exception noted at the conclusion of this paper.

upon their fellowmen, and especially to protect the weak from the powerful.

II. These moral concepts together cause us to ask the statesmen of the world to give intensified consideration to their application to the contemporary crisis in world affairs through steps such as these:

A. Modernize the United Nations through Article 109 of the Charter, so that a new and more effective United Nations might emerge from the old, encompassing within it all of the peoples of the world.

B. Establish improved institutions for peace-making and improved police forces for peace-keeping such as:

1. A United Nations Board of Arbitration.
2. A United Nations Panel of Mediators.
3. A World Court for equitable and just peaceful solutions.
4. A dependable method of financial support for United Nations peace-keeping institutions.
5. An elite police force of volunteers serving directly in a United Nations police force, both armed and unarmed.

C. If necessary, for effective representation of all peoples in this contemporary period of history, invite into the United Nations two member governments each for the people of Germany, China, Vietnam, and Korea.

D. Make deliberate moves to stop at once the bombing of North Vietnam; to quiet down and de-escalate the war in Vietnam; to accept both Vietnamese governments into the United Nations; to place a United Nations police force between the North and South; to insure a cessation of hostilities on both sides; to safeguard an honorable ending of the war through new United Nations or Geneva Conference solutions; and to rebuild the war damage in both North and South Vietnam.

E. Take further initiatives with these objectives: to assist the peoples of the Mideast to turn to peaceful development of resources and away from war; to safeguard the

just rights and secure the existence of all peoples and of all
member states of the United Nations in the area; and to
provide for full respect and adequate access to all of the
historic shrines of all religions.

F. Carry out, preferably through the United Nations
and other multilateral methods, a vast expansion of resources devoted to human progress in food, shelter, clothing, health, and educational opportunities for all humanity
on this earth; and a sharp decline in resources devoted to
armaments, through reciprocal limitations, inspections, and
controls.

G. Endeavor through the non-aligned countries at this
particular time to reach a major broad *détente* so as to end
the cold war on a basis which will advance worldwide
development, trade, security, and peace.

H. Persist in negotiations on all international disputes,
mindful of the numerous successful settlements through
negotiations, too often overlooked.

III. We respectfully petition religious leaders around the
world to review and contemplate the premises and the spe-
cifics of this report:

A. We believe that in this hour the world search for
peace would be enhanced by the extension, on both a
regional and a worldwide basis, of the dialogue conducted
at this Symposium, and ultimately by a World Association
of Religions for Peace. This consideration should include
the previous work and resolutions in the area of inter-
religious meetings and efforts for peace.

B. We submit this report as an initial endeavor to bring
into focus the combined moral viewpoint which seems to
us to be an imperative in the urgent world search for the
way of peace with justice and freedom.

C. We convey to them our sense of urgent need of affirmative and intelligent action for peace.

D. We recommend that, even in times of conflict, governments should allow religious leaders throughout the

world to communicate with one another to seek mediation toward peace.

E. We invite and will welcome their mobilization of support, and their future participation in our continued efforts, as individuals or as organized groups or as religious bodies.

IV. We urge peoples of the nations of the world, east and west, north and south, of all races and of all religions, to encourage and sustain the constructive efforts for peace on the part of their leaders of state and of all religions and of all occupations. We invite participation in the process of thinking through and of acting upon the possibilities of peace founded upon the universal moral precepts commonly held by the major religions of the world.

V. We appeal to the communication media around the world: the press, radio, television, and other forms of publication, for the service they perform in conveying the thoughts and objectives of this report to people and to leaders on all continents, recognizing that only through these media can there be the essential rapidity and comprehensiveness of communication.

VI. We ask the leaders of the Symposium to present personally and respectfully a copy of the conclusions to the Secretary-General of the United Nations, the Honorable U Thant, and to heads of government at their discretion where appropriate.

The chairman of the religious board of the Buddhists of the U.S.S.R., Jambel D. Gomboev, presents the attached separate note of dissent and an alternate proposal on the subject of this panel.

The Delegation of the Buddhists of the U.S.S.R., having considered the draft working paper on peace-making and peace-keeping, suggests the following amendments:

1. All the proposals specified in II A, B, C, D, and E should be dropped, because Section II A and B deal with ques-

tions to modernize and strengthen the United Nations, to establish peace-making and peace-improving international institutions like the United Nations Board of Arbitration, the United Nations Panel of Mediators, a World Court for Equitable and Just Peaceful Solutions, and a United Nations police force.

Dealing with such questions, the Panel on Peace-Making and Peace-Keeping of the International Inter-Religious Symposium on Peace takes upon itself the responsibility to solve international political questions from the viewpoint of interest of certain states, while such questions should be considered only at an international forum where all the countries and states are duly represented by accredited representatives.

Secondly, questions about the representation in the United Nations of such countries as Germany, China, Vietnam, and Korea cannot be considered by the participants of the Symposium, for the reason that they are not represented at the Symposium. Besides, each of these countries requires special consideration.

Thirdly, the draft resolution regarding the deescalation of the war in Vietnam answers neither to the interests of the Vietnamese people nor to the desire of religions to promote sanctions for peace. Neither does it answer the spirit of those speeches which were delivered at the Symposium. Furthermore, it does not demand the cessation of war, but it suggests the retention of aggressive troops which is more a program for further aggressive actions.

The Delegation of Buddhists of the U.S.S.R. suggests the following proposals:

1. In accordance with the Geneva Agreement on Vietnam, the following steps should be taken immediately: Stop the bombing of North Vietnam, stop military activities in South Vietnam, withdraw all foreign troops from the country, give an opportunity to the Vietnamese

people to exercise their rights to decide by themselves their own future.

2. Take effective steps to reestablish peace and security in the Middle East: Condemn the Israeli aggression against the Arabs, demand the withdrawal of Israeli troops from occupied territory, and return the unlawfully occupied territories to the Arab States.

3. Appeal to religious leaders of the world to call upon people to join efforts to safeguard and strengthen peace all over the world.

3. ⚘ INAUGURAL PAPERS

THE SYMPOSIUM OPENED in the great hall of the India International Center on January 10, 1968. Dr. Zakir Husain, President of India, gave the inaugural address. His words were heard not only by participants and observers of the Symposium, but by invited guests from the Delhi region, especially representatives from a number of religious groups. Shri R. R. Diwakar, President of the Gandhi Peace Foundation, was chairman. The session began with a Gandhian religious service, including liturgical materials from several world religions. After a welcome address by Shri G. Ramachandran, secretary of the Gandhi Peace Foundation, keynote addresses were made by Shri Jayaprakash Narayan and Bishop John Wesley Lord. The inaugural meeting ended with a word of thanks and of hope by Dr. Homer A. Jack. Following this first session, there was a reception and tea for participants and observers. The papers given at this inaugural session, except that of President Husain which constitutes the preface of this volume, are given below.

Shri R. R. Diwakar, M.P.

WORLD PEACE, peace between nations, can no longer continue to be the concern of a few rulers, governments, politicians,

statesmen, or military experts. It is not at all safe or secure in their hands. They seem to be experts only in keeping real peace away, perpetuating the present state of near war, and continuing the most dangerous preparations for war.

A war or wars, declared or undeclared, and in whatever corner of the world they may be fought, disturb the peace of every country and physically and mentally affect all nations and peoples. Even the smallest war cannot be called a local war because it disturbs the whole equilibrium and structure of world peace. Peace and war are therefore indivisible and have to be considered as phenomena which are of concern to the whole of humanity.

It is also necessary to look at war from the new point of view of the manufacture and stockpiling of murderous and destructive weapons—nuclear, chemical, biological, and other. These are capable of wiping out all life and human civilization from the surface of this earth. The uninvolved thus have as much stake in war and peace as the participants, since war means interminable suffering and death while peace is the very essential condition of life, progress, and happiness.

There is a third very important reason why real peace is the precondition for the happy and healthy existence of the people. The continuance of the cold war, with a hot war round the corner, acts as a corroding and disturbing factor. It produces an uncanny fear and undermines the sense of security which is necessary for peace of mind and healthy functioning.

War and peace must be the concern not only of constituted political authorities, but of every man and woman who is capable of thinking and acting. The machinery such as the United Nations, set up by politicians, has so far failed to maintain peace except in a very small way in isolated instances. The initiative for peace and war still rests with the constituted political authorities in each country. Unless overwhelming, massive, and universal sanctions are created for

peace and against war by the citizens of each country, there is no hope of real peace being established. Such sanctions can come about only when we all realize that the whole of the human species is one single community and that we are on the march in the mighty adventure of life, as it seeks to reach new heights of evolution, leading to universal peace, harmony, and happiness. Thanks to science and technology, and the rapidly developing means of communication, the realization of the oneness of humanity and life itself need not any longer be the monopoly of saints and men gifted with spiritual perception, but it can be experienced in our daily lives as we open the morning paper and listen to the radio. Man's consciousness, an individual's awareness today, is not that of an isolated soul imprisoned in the shell of the tabernacle and cursed with narrow egoism. Man's mind is now receptive and responsive to whatever good or bad that happens to any human being in any corner of the world.

Man has not only developed a very vast, extensive, and deep consciousness of things, but he is also self-conscious. He not only knows, but also knows that he knows. He is capable of knowing not merely what is going on outside his body and mind, but of knowing what is going on within his own mind. He has a "without" as well as a "within" and he lives and moves and has his being in both these worlds, which are interwoven with and which interpenetrate each other. He has the gift of introspection. In virtue of this, he has developed the faculty of conscience, of judging what is good and what is bad. He can reject the bad and accept the good. He can refuse to follow the path of evil and tread the path that leads to good. In the course of evolution, he is no longer a mere toy to be tossed about in the hands of blind cosmic forces. Man has come of age. To that extent he is the master of destiny. He must now play his part boldly, heroically, and wisely so that he can elevate himself to the next stage of evolution. His is and ought to be now a course of conscious,

self-guided evolution towards higher and nobler reaches of humanity, nearer and nearer to divinity.

It is but natural that this responsibility, at this juncture, of shaping our future to the extent that we can should devolve on the leaders of thought and action in the human community. Our minds, therefore, turn more to religious institutions and heads, and to those who have dedicated their lives to walking in the path of religion, than to others.

For what is religion if it is not every urge, aspiration, and emotion, every thought and system of thought and idea, every action and guideline of conduct and relationship which leads and lifts and enables man and human society to turn away from falsehood and untruth towards truth, from darkness and ignorance towards light and knowledge, from disease and death towards health and immortality, from hatred and war towards love and peace, from the path of destruction towards that of construction. The very essence and mission of religion is to take us from where we are to purer and nobler regions where egoism is replaced with altruism, where service is greater than self, where love and identity are the ruling emotions. It is the very breath and inspiration of religion to give us the strength to wean ourselves away from everything that leads to war and to promote everything that makes us live in friendliness, mutual understanding, and cooperation—in a word, in peace.

But what is peace? Let us not restrict the meaning of this great word only to the absence of war, of war tensions, or of war psychosis. Peace is neither only the absence of war nor even only the precondition for all friendliness. It is not a state of restfulness or inactivity. It is a potent dynamism itself, it is coiled power poised to spring into action for further progress and for a determined fight against ignorance, sloth, poverty, meanness, and everything that clogs the path of man to greatness and glory and to sublime achievement. While speaking of world peace and goodwill among nations, let us, therefore, not forget the wider significance and the utter necessity of peace between man and man, between religion and religion, between group and group—that great peace which is the very matrix of all noble activity and which is creative and formative of the future of humanity.

Man cannot be partly hating and partly loving, partly at peace and partly at war. That psychological illusion must now give place to establishing a total climate of peace in our own minds as well as among those in the midst of whom we live and move. Only such a grand endeavor as this on the part of man can ensure the abolition of the barbarous method of war as a solution to the problems arising out of conflicts of interest and demoniac ambitions to exploit and dominate over others on the sheer strength of physical power. Power divorced from morality and the dictates of human conscience is at the root of the struggle for power and dominance. The function of morality, of man's conscience, and of the religious instinct in man is to reform humanity and usher in the age of peace, love, and cooperation.

It is undoubtedly the major responsibility of all religions to put forth their best efforts to establish peace at all levels, because no religion—formal, doctrinal, or ritualistic—can be practiced properly without inner as well as outer peace. The essence of every religion is to seek the truth and, having found it, to live and establish it at all costs. It is another matter that sometimes individual seekers come into conflict with institutional religious authority and have to suffer as a result. The depth and degree of faith in truth and the relentless search for it is the greatest adventure that a human soul can launch upon. Truth alone is in fact the highest value to a pure and selfless spirit imbued with the essence of religion. Truth is that which the whole soul, the total being, believes to be true; truth is identical with the facts of experience to which the senses, the mind, and the conscience are witness. But the religious spirit does not stop at only recognizing and knowing truth; the truly religious spirit earnestly endeavors with all its might to realize truth in its whole being and action. It counts no cost too great in this supreme effort and is ready to sacrifice everything it holds dear, pleasant, and attractive, including the seductive pleasures of the flesh, of the senses, and of even the mind. Its drive and its one aim is to identify itself with the very source of all existence and that which makes life itself worth living.

History tells us that many of the great world religions were founded by noble individual souls who had the vision of truth and concern for the future of humanity. Mighty institutions of such religions continue to flourish and to do their noble task. But what seems necessary today is something more than this—a concentrated effort for peace by a kind of united religious organization of the whole world. A reorientation of the whole life of man towards mutual love, understanding, and peace, and a serious attempt towards achieving a one world and world government are the demands of the day. A world without war and the whole of humanity at peace have to be the ideal of all. That alone can take us nearer the goal and be called a substantial contribution to the cherished hope of peace on earth and goodwill among men. Only a peaceful world will help realize the dream of *visva-kutumba:* "The world as one family."

Shri Jayaprakash Narayan

I AM NOT A RELIGIOUS MAN in the traditional sense of the term and I have no right to speak to the representatives of the different religions who are gathered here to discuss the vital question of peace. However, I shall present to you a picture, not of the world, but of India as I see it.

India is no doubt the land of the Buddha, Mahavira, Gandhi, and other great teachers of love and compassion. But

we would be very mistaken if we assumed therefore that
India today is a country which values peace or that its people
are living a life of peace. As I see the picture around me, the
reality is just the opposite. We have violence all over the
country and we have violence of all kinds. We have political
violence; we have communal and caste violence. Recently we
had not only four communal riots in Bihar—Hindu-Muslim
riots—but also two caste riots between two predominant
castes, riots which took their origin in the two universities of
Bihar. This is the picture for you of the so-called elite of our
society, the educated people who go to the universities,
whether they are teachers or students. There would seem to
be more violence in our hearts and minds today than we
realize. I do not think I have overdrawn the picture.

If we turn from the internal situation to the international
question in which we as a country are involved, we find that
we have had disputes with our two neighbors, Pakistan and
China. Here again, I noticed the same temper in the country,
the same kind of hostility, the same impatience with people
who talk of any kind of peaceful settlement.

The question which I think is relevant for this Symposium
is this: Where are the religions of India in this picture? What
role are they playing? We have all the great religions of the
world represented in India. Some of them such as Hinduism,
Buddhism, and certain other smaller religions originated from
this soil. Indeed, India is a country of religions. And then
in history it has been found that most of these religions have
lived together, if not in fellowship, at least in a spirit of
mutuality, of live and let live. There have been few religious
wars in India.

Today the religions in India, to put it at the mildest, do not
seem to be even concerned with the questions of peace, internal or external. I would like to make an exception of the
Christian religion, and that merely because the Christian community here is a part of the world Christian community and

is influenced by whatever peace movements are taking place in the wombs of the churches to which they belong. As for the rest, except for rare individual religious leaders or such rare religious organizations or orders as the Ramakrishna Mission, they do not seem to be concerned with these questions. And these questions are vital, not only for world peace, but also for ourselves, for our survival, for our progress, for our prosperity, for the happiness of the children who are growing up and who will be the next generation in India, the citizens of the future.

I should like to ask myself why this is so. Firstly, even though there are many religions in India, the majority of Indians are Hindus. The Hindu religion, as is true of Islam today, is not an organized religion in the sense in which the Christians understand the term or the West understands the term. I think the sentiment of the Hindus—I am not saying their thinking, but just their sentiment—is something like the following. The Hindus have lived for centuries, except perhaps for the past five centuries, under Muslim political domination. There were periods during that time when there was also Muslim religious domination. For a century at least after the Muslims left, and for nearly two centuries in some parts of the country if we reckon the time from the Battle of Plassey, the Hindus lived under the domination of a Christian nation, and in many ways under the domination of the Christian religion, which was the favored religion at that time even though the British did not practice religious persecution of any kind. One might say that the British did not practice religious persecution consciously, although unconsciously they did certainly practice religious discrimination. Nonetheless this fact of domination for centuries has been there and it has, I think, chastened the Hindu mind.

With the achievement of freedom, the natural reaction of the Hindu has been to assert himself, and to assert himself in an aggressive and sectarian manner. When we were fighting for the freedom of this country under our great leaders, from Raja Ram Mohan Roy to Mahatma Gandhi, the very terms of that struggle dictated that all the communities seriously concerned should unite to fight the common enemy. As a result, at the end of that period a sense of unity was created. But that sense of unity was not so deep as to prevent the partition of the country on the very eve of its independence.

The need for that kind of unity now seems to have disappeared, and among those who formed the majority in this country and who had a stake in their religion, Hindu nationalism began to grow, in alliance with aggressive Hindu religious sectarianism. We find its expression in the political field, in the student world, in cultural spheres, and almost everywhere. For a man like me, this is a suicidal development. If it is allowed to run its course unchecked, this country will break up as it broke up at the time of independence. But, with a few exceptions, I do not see the religious organizations, whether Hindu or any other, concerning themselves with this problem. In fact the emphasis seems to be on the other side.

Now we turn to our secular state. It is certainly of great social, cultural, and political value that we have accepted secularism as our way of civic and political life. It is obvious to me that the forces of secularism are now on the retreat. Even in the field of politics, the secular parties are not joining issue with those which are frankly antisecular.

If we turn from the internal scene to the external, we find much the same kind of attitude. I worked as a member of the Nagaland Peace Mission. In Nagaland they practice certain forms of tribal religion and tribal worship. If the Hindu religion is prepared to call these unconverted, unchristian people of Nagaland Hindus, perhaps the definition of the word Hindu will have to be made much wider than it already is. You know how difficult it is to define who a Hindu is. A Hindu is the end product of an organic growth of thousands of years of evolution, adjustment, and reconciliation. Whenever we speak of the Naga question, immediately the religious leaders' reaction is that it is a plot prepared by the Christian missionary and foreign powers to cut Nagaland off from India. While the Christian religion has tried in the past to work in these neglected areas and has brought to the people culture, education, health, and other social services, you will look in vain for any religious Hindu organization working towards the same end. But immediately the cry will be raised that only ten percent of the people in Nagaland are Christians and that the rest are Hindus. If you wish to call them Hindus, they are beef eating Hindus because beef and pork are the mainstays of their diet. Once I was nearly mobbed by a crowd when I said that in ancient days even the Hindus ate beef.

The history of the last hundreds of years in India is like a heavy load on our mind. We cannot also forget that it is not a properly understood, properly presented, or properly written history. It is a distorted kind of history; it is one-sided history, mostly written by others. The immediate reaction to such history was to glorify everything. But now probably there is a more objective attitude developing among historians.

In the talks that are to follow today and in the next few days, religious leaders will tell the Symposium what the sanctions for peace are in their own religions. I daresay every religion has those sanctions. But I do not see those sanctions taking us toward the goal of peace, and that is the problem. I hope the outcome of this Symposium will lead us toward peace.

As a Hindu, I sometimes hope for another Vivekananda to be born to present to the Hindus themselves the best of their own religion. Every religion, as every individual, has both its depths and its heights. The question before religions is whether it is their divisive, exclusive aspects that are going to be emphasized or their synoptic aspects. All the great religions proclaim the fatherhood of one God and the brotherhood of man. But having proclaimed this as an abstraction, when it comes to down-to-earth existence in the different communities in India, you will find the religions dividing and creating barriers, often in villages where Hindus and Muslims live together. At one time perhaps there was no communication between them as inter-religious communities, but today there is much less than there was fifty years ago. Therefore, some effort has to be made to increase communication between them and the initiative that has been taken here in this Symposium is a wonderful beginning.

I hope the Symposium will address itself to the role of religious groups, organizations, and leaders in the task of achieving peace—international peace. This is not a philosophical or moral question for us; it is a question of national survival. At one time, when the great religions were born and spread all over the world, they pledged to bring nations and races together under the umbrella of all embracing religion. But around the time of the industrial revolution, the revolution itself and certain other socioeconomic forces that were developing in the womb of European society led to the establishment of the nation-state, before which all the religions seem to be powerless. The day of the nation-state is past. In this age of science, everyone talks, as President Husain did talk, of the one-world community. But the fact remains—and it is a very horrifying fact—as the Inter-Religious Conference in Washington has said in its declaration, that the Christian church and religion twice failed to prevent two great wars. This is the same all over the world. Whereas religion should unite humanity, it is one of the strongest divisive forces today; and when religion is linked with the nation-state, then the danger of divisiveness is multiplied tenfold.

All that I have done is to present to you the picture in India and I am sure that religions, religious leaders, and religious organizations have a great and very vital role to play. It is for them to decide whether they will play that role or not.

Bishop John Wesley Lord

WE ARE GATHERED HERE to explore ways and means by which the leaders and followers of the great world religions can work for the establishment of peace within a nation and between and among nations. Such a gathering may well represent a breakthrough to peace, and mark a milestone in the preparation for the Gandhi Centenary Celebrations in India and the rest of the world in 1969.

The significance of this breakthrough is heightened by the confession that many times throughout history religious differences have been the contributing factors in the rise of international conflicts and the waging of war. From the days of the Crusades and before, to the recent weeks and months of the year that has ended, we have seen the exploitation of religious feeling and witnessed once again the role of religious antagonism as a factor in the appeal to war. It is imperative that during the days of this Symposium, we be on our guard lest our religious idealism become a factor in promoting war.

It needs also to be observed that the religious faiths represented here have differing concepts of peace. It will be the purpose of this Symposium to discover and explore these concepts with the hope that, through understanding and synthesis, we shall create the climate for constructive dialogue not alone among ourselves but among those in our world who are the honest unbelievers, the communist world included. We will need the courage and integrity to review with special moral vigilance the activities and achievements toward peace in those groups to which we give our first loyalties. This could

prove to be a very humbling experience, for in too many instances we have substituted an aversion to war for the will to
peace. A simple aversion to war may very easily become a
contributing factor to war. Let me quote Bishop John J.
Wright of Pittsburgh on this matter:

> A mere aversion to war often reveals itself only in the acute
> crises that threaten us from time to time; when the crises
> pass, we do not have attendance at parleys like this. Our job
> is to help build the love for peace that must motivate and sus-
> tain the work of religious moral education, beginning with
> ourselves, as well as the work of social justice, beginning with
> the other fellow. At the same time, we have the task of re-
> maining faithful to the imperatives of moral wisdom.

We must possess an efficacious will for peace that is marked
by an unqualified, total commitment to all that peace requires.
There are few in our day who either understand or who are
prepared to pay the price that peace demands. We choose
rather to feel that peace is simply the absence of war. This is
sheer folly and dangerous as well. Peace may be as costly as
war itself, but its achievements will bless and not curse mankind. We must "spell out" our devotion to peace.

With these confessions and laments behind us, we set the
stage to fulfill the high hopes of our Symposium, namely, that
this conference "prepare the way for a spirit of mutual understanding between followers of different religions in the
pursuit of the goal of peace and also foster a sense of urgency
in the supreme task of doing something in the name of religion,
in the name of all that we hold sacred, to preserve peace and
maintain it for the good of mankind as a whole."

The late President of the United States, John F. Kennedy,
on occasion reminded the religious leaders of the nation that
the basic problems facing us were moral and spiritual problems, and that all the military could do was to provide us
time to get the job done. Whatever we may make of this

statement, we must admit that the religious forces of mankind are involved in the problems of mankind. If we cannot bring peace, we can prevent it. May God grant us the wisdom and the will to create peace and not destroy it.

We are gathered at this Symposium, and at considerable expense to all participants, because we believe that the most critical and urgent problem facing mankind today is the monstrosity of another world war that grows more menacing with each passing day. Therefore, the challenge we face here is building defenses of peace. "Since wars begin in the minds of men, it is in the minds of men that the defenses of peace must be constructed." Can we do it? Can we destroy the myths that have plagued mankind since time began?

Is it not reasonable to conclude that, since we deal so largely with the training and developing of the minds of men, we have a most sacred obligation to forcefully, intelligently, and spiritually lead those minds to consider the causes of war and the means to peace? The answer must be in the affirmative.

We are appalled at the intellectual burden of peace. Those who have labored longest and hardest for the goal now admit that all we can do is direct our efforts "toward" peace. This Symposium may reveal the need for further and sustained effort on a new level and in new areas of human concern. Perhaps peace is best conceived as a process, in which step by step we meet the conditions required of us. The *shalom* (Hebrew word for peace) of the Bible is rich in meaning and refers primarily to the concern for blessedness, wholeness, prosperity, safety, welfare, happiness, and security. This peace involves the relationship between God and his community. Biblical peace is not private, but collective, social, and public. Individual peace is based upon the peace of the community. While peace is the free gift of God, it also involves man's obedience to his commandments.

Nor can we make a sharp distinction between the establish-

ment of peace and justice. Because God's justice and peace
are integrally related, our struggle for peace cannot be successful if we do not struggle at the same time for justice. Both
have the same imperative in the commandment of love. There
will be no true and lasting peace without justice in freedom.
A peace based on obvious injustice is not Biblical peace.

Perhaps this truth could be affirmed by many groups in the
West now dealing with peace and international problems. Indeed, it is in the very acceptance of this basic premise in the
West that we are brought face to face with the Christian's
dilemma. In the evil and sinful society of which we are a
part, the dual striving for justice and peace often confronts us
with the necessity to accept either the use of force or the suffering of our fellow men. Some Christian disciples keep peace
by choosing to endure suffering themselves rather than inflict
it on others.

My intention at this point is to reveal the relative progress
we are making in the West, while recognizing that our best
is not good enough. We pray not for an easy peace but for a
lasting one; we ask not simply for a cessation of bombing or
battle but for the cessation of the need for war; not for the
removal of strain and anxiety but for the ability to handle
strain and anxiety in our daily living; not for an end of responsibility but for the facility to assume more; not simply
order in our cities, but for order in our lives.

Order in our lives I would place as the number one need
of the West. Pride and self-righteousness are prime obstacles
to peace among men as among nations. In his tribute to the
United Nations, His Holiness, Pope Paul VI, urging that
attention be given to the revision of the charter of the United
Nations, said this:

The reason for this wish, which might be said to pertain to
the structure of your organization, leads us to complete it
with other formulas. They are these: let no one, as a member

of your association, be superior to the others; not one above another. This is the formula of equality. We well know that there are other factors to be considered besides that of mere membership in this body. But equality too is part of its constitution; not that you are equal, but that you make yourselves equal. And it may be that for several among you this is an act of high virtue; allow us to say this to you, we who represent a religion which works salvation through the humility of its divine Founder. It is impossible to be a brother, if one is not humble. For it is pride, however inevitable it may seem, which provides tensions, struggles for prestige, predominance, colonialism, selfishness; it is pride that shatters brotherhood.

It could be the presence of pride in this Symposium that could shatter and dispel the dreams and high hopes of our committee. The problem of the individual is a microcosm of the problem of the nation. God must forgive our pride and arrogance.

We do "reaffirm our faith in fundamental human rights, in the dignity and worth of the human person, in equal rights of men and women and of nations large and small, and we are determined to establish conditions under which justice and respect for the obligations arising from treaties and other sources of international law can be maintained, and to promote social progress and better standards of life in larger freedom." I could wish that all over the world, religious groups might offer more positive support of the United Nations and become more vocal in its behalf. It appears to many as our one great hope for a structured peace in our world. The Prophet Isaiah reminds us that "out of Zion shall go forth the law, and the word of the Lord from Jerusalem." It becomes an exercise in futility to hope for peace in our world unless and until there exists a structure in law that can sustain peace in principle and justice. Many workers in the cause of peace in the West would accept this reality.

But how far we have come is expressed by Dr. Bronislaw Bilinski of the Polish Academy of Sciences at Rome, in an address given last summer at New York University:

> The old idea voiced by Horace that war is a natural, normal part of social well-being has been and must continue to be reversed. In the ancient world war was glorified. Now we must believe that it is not glorious to die, but glorious to live. As Erasmus said, "War is noble to those who know nothing about it." We must now promote war, not as normal, but as abnormal, social behavior.

Not religion alone, but religion together with the social sciences and the humanities must seek to change the nature and direction of society, so that together with the scientists religious leaders may use their skills in solving social problems and bring into being a greater humanity. The purpose of this Symposium and those to come must be to launch a massive intellectual effort in peace research.

Shri G. Ramachandran, M.P.

WE ARE ASSEMBLED HERE TODAY for this Symposium as believers in God and as members of various religions from many countries. The first poignant memory, however, that comes to my mind, as I welcome you, is that this is the city of Delhi in which Mahatma Gandhi gave up his life for the cause of goodwill and peace between Muslims and Hindus and therefore among all men everywhere. We are meeting together now to advance the same cause in our own countries and in the world as a whole. The cause is a very big one and we are only a few humble people working for it in this Symposium. Therefore we can derive the necessary strength and courage only from God, and that only if we are worthy. What can bind us together is the divine teaching in each one of our religious traditions that the law of God is the law of love and that only the law of love can produce nonviolence and peace.

There must be no doubt in our minds that for us peace and nonviolence are convertible terms. The challenge to us in this century is to prove that men of the various religions in the world can work together more sincerely and more courageously for peace than can any other group of people anywhere. This is why we must sit together in a spirit of harmony, dedication, and enterprise during the brief days of this Symposium. Gandhi defined nonviolence as love in action. Wherever love acts it can act only in terms of nonviolence. We have therefore to prove in the modern world, which is on the brink of great peril from vast and unprecedented armaments including stockpiles of nuclear weapons, that love can become nonviolent action and that nonviolent action can lead to world peace.

Mahatma Gandhi was neither the first nor is he going to be the last of the prophets of nonviolence and peace. Behind Gandhi we trace the colossal figures of Buddha, Jesus, Mohammed, Zoroaster, Mahavira, Nanak, and others. But equally, there also stand behind Gandhi the mighty figures of the fighters for human freedom like Lincoln, Sun Yat-sen, Lenin, Nehru, Martin Luther King, Jr., and others. It is this synthesis of nonviolence and human freedom which is the greatest gift of Gandhi to mankind. Gandhi contradicted the central truth of no religion nor the passion for any political or social freedom but confirmed and fulfilled in his own way both these inescapable urges of the human spirit. Gandhi held that peace and justice were the two sides of the same coin and one could not exist without the other. He never sacrificed justice for peace or peace for justice. Both were equally valid in his concept and practice of truth and nonviolence. We must keep this dynamic synthesis as we labor together in this Symposium for peace as representatives of different religions.

This Symposium is being held under the joint auspices of the U.S. Inter-Religious Committee on Peace and the Seminars

Committee of the Gandhi Centenary Committee. But in a deeper sense the sponsors are the representatives of the many religions gathered here and also the many observers who have come to add strength to the representatives. I welcome them all most sincerely. Let me add that the Gandhi Peace Foundation is sharing considerably in the responsibility of conducting this Symposium. My welcome therefore is also on behalf of the Gandhi Peace Foundation.

It is now my special and respectful privilege to welcome Dr. Zakir Husain, the President of the Republic of India. "Zakir Sahib," as we affectionately call him, has by his association with us today added greatly to the stature and reality of this Symposium. Even if he were not the President of the Republic of India, he would have been equally welcome as one of the noblest Muslims this country has produced and as a devotee of God with invincible faith that the will of God continues to guide mankind from one great destiny to another. We welcome him with all our hearts. May I add a special word of welcome to Shri R. R. Diwakar, chairman of the Gandhi Peace Foundation, who is also the chairman of this inaugural function of the Symposium. His presence here today is to us the guarantee of the moral support of the Gandhi Peace Foundation. And then, we could not have had a worthier representative of the composite culture of India and of Mahatma Gandhi and Acharya Vinoba than Shri Jayaprakash Narayan who is one of the keynote speakers this afternoon. I bracket with him Bishop John Wesley Lord from the United States, whose renown has preceded his arrival in India. In Swami Ranganathananda, who will speak today on the "Sanctions for World Peace in Hinduism," we have a man of profound spirituality and great learning. I offer my welcome to this trinity of our speakers today.

I am afraid we shall have to cultivate the art of brevity in our speeches and discussions during the Symposium. We have many distinguished speakers, and many important subjects to discuss. Unless we voluntarily and scrupulously keep to the time limit, we shall not be able to cover all the subjects in proper time and to arrive at worthwhile conclusions. We must also demonstrate that men of religion can discuss every problem of world peace without acrimony and in a spirit of complete harmony and gentleness. I have no doubt in my mind we shall pass all these tests without a strain.

May I then welcome particularly all those who will read papers and participate in the discussions. Let us hope that by the time we reach our concluding session we shall have fully done the work we have planned to do. We should be able to present at the concluding session findings and decisions which will help us to proceed, step by step, in every country and in every religious constituency from which we have come, towards organizing and strengthening the urgent and inescapable momentum for world peace. Let us prove that our religious constituencies can and will respond more effectively and swiftly than our political or national constituencies all over the world to the call for world peace.

Before I conclude, let me add that it has been a privilege to work in the preparation for this Symposium with Dr. Homer A. Jack of the U.S. Inter-Religious Committee on Peace as a fellow secretary of the Symposium. He has already given many of us invaluable lessons in American efficiency, generosity, and depth of understanding.

May we all now march into the work of the Symposium keeping the name of God on our lips and his image, as each one of us understands it, in our hearts.

Homer A. Jack

IT IS MY PLEASANT DUTY to offer thanks at this conclusion of the inaugural session of this historic International Inter-Religious Symposium on Peace.

We deeply appreciate both the presence of Dr. Zakir
Husain, President of India, and the message he has given us.
We who happen to be non-Indians, even those of us who
represent organized religions, are deeply impressed by the
secular nature of the Indian state. We were particularly impressed some months ago when Dr. Husain was elected to the
presidency of India. And now we are impressed by his
person and by what he has told us. Indeed, when Dr. Husain
was still Vice-President of India, Mr. Halbert and I had the
privilege of talking to him about the hopes of the U.S. Inter-
Religious Committee on Peace for a symposium on religion
and peace. He gave us every encouragement. So it is fitting
that, now that he is President of India, he is attending our
opening function. We are additionally honored that he is
inviting all delegates and observers at this Symposium to the
Rashtrapathi Bhawan for a reception.

We are also grateful for the deep interest the Gandhi
Memorial Trust, the Gandhi Centenary Committee, and the
Gandhi Peace Foundation are taking in this Symposium. Shri
R. R. Diwakar is involved in all three institutions and it is
proper that he be chairman of this inaugural session. As chairman, he gave us a penetrating address. Shri Diwakar is a leader
in the true Gandhian tradition and it is a pleasure that he leads
this gathering this day.

Shri Jayaprakash Narayan has become a legend to some
of us overseas admirers of India during its first two decades
of independence. Although Jayaprakash took his university
training in the United States and is soon to visit America
again, we know him mostly from afar. But what we know we
like. He is a true, courageous prophet in the best tradition of
both Gandhi and Vinoba. And so we implored him to give
one of the two keynote speeches at this inaugural session.
Jayaprakash is not, to be sure, a person relating to any one
organized religion. We selected him just because we who are
of church, synagogue, temple, or mosque need the realism,

the critique, the prophecy of the broad outlook. Jayaprakash has given this to us.

Bishop John Wesley Lord is head of the American delegation at this Symposium. He is a dynamic, respected bishop of the Methodist church in the United States capital, Washington. Today he reflected the best of the Christian church—universal and militant—in his keynote address.

Swami Ranganathananda I first met in Calcutta last February when we acquainted him with our hopes for an inter-religious conference on peace. He agreed to our recent invitation to present the first of a series of papers at this Symposium on the sanctions of various world religions, their scriptures, and their traditions for world peace. His address was scholarly, and yet we were able to follow and enjoy it and profit from it —always assets at conferences of learned men of religion.

Shri G. Ramachandran, M.P., has been my colleague as joint secretary of this Symposium. We have worked as brothers ever since I visited him last September in south India at his remarkable community of Gandhigram. Since I returned to India in mid-December, we have worked closely with his staff at the Gandhi Peace Foundation. In the process I have found my own passage to India and it is not unlike my own office on Beacon Hill in Boston. Indeed, I am kidnaping several functionaries at the Gandhi Peace Foundation to take back with me to America. We might kidnap G. Ramachandran himself and have him enrich the upper house of the American parliament—the Senate—as surely he must the Rajya Sabha here in New Delhi.

As you know, this Symposium is the first seminar of the Gandhi Centenary programs running from early 1968 through 1970—three years. It is right that this Symposium on religion and peace be called in the spirit of that great world leader. Back in 1928, Gandhiji wrote that "the aim should be to help a Hindu to become a better Hindu, a Mussalman to become a better Mussalman, and a Christian a better Christian."

Even earlier, in 1925, Gandhiji wrote that "religion which takes no account of practical affairs and does not help to solve them is no religion." Elsewhere he said that "the prime practical goal of mankind is to put an end to war." In this spirit, our friends on this platform have inaugurated this historic Symposium. Thank you all once again for making the inaugural function an inspiring success.

4. ✍ SANCTIONS FOR PEACE (I)

THOSE PLANNING THE SYMPOSIUM early realized that one of the most important aspects would be the presentation by leaders of the major religions represented of the sanctions for peace of their respective religious traditions. This was not to be a conference on comparative religion, but rather a symposium on how various religions assessed the common human problem of peace. Accordingly, representatives of a number of religions read papers on this topic. At the inaugural session Swami Ranganathananda discussed the Hindu sanctions for peace. At the second session four other such papers were given. This session was chaired by Princess Poon Pismal Diskul, president of the World Fellowship of Buddhists. It opened with a Buddhist service, with several monks participating, including eighty-two-year-old Rev. G. Nichidatsu Fujii of Japan, who was associated with Mahatma Gandhi. After all four papers were presented, there was a short discussion period.

HINDUISM
Swami Ranganathananda

A STUDY OF THE AIMS AND OBJECTS of religion reveals it to be essentially a discipline for peace. Yet even a cursory study of the history of religion shows that all the religions of the world have contributed to war as much as to peace in varying degrees. Every religion emphasizes the need to discipline the forces of lust and greed and other passions in man which are the sources of violence and war outside. All religions emphasize the brotherhood of man, and some of them the fatherhood of God as well. All religions have contributed immensely to the integration of man with man in society and to the development of human culture and civilization.

Why then do religions, which function as constructive forces for integration and peace within their respective social groups, become transformed into destructive forces of intolerance, violence, and war when they step out of their respective social milieus? How to convert them into constructive forces even outside their own respective groups? These are the two main problems which every religion today has to face and to solve so that there may be a confluence of the world's spiritual resources strong and pure enough to liberate modern man from the prevailing soul-killing worldliness and restore him to his spiritual integrity and glory.

Indian spiritual tradition recognizes the presence in every religion of two sets of truths, one essential, eternal, and universal, and the other nonessential, temporary, and parochial. The former is called *sruti*, constituting the essential core of spiritual insights, and hence called *sanatana dharma* (eternal religion), and the latter *smṛti*, which seeks to embody these insights in personal laws and social institutions, is called *yuga dharma* (religion for a particular age), the scope of which is limited. India therefore upholds the primacy of the *sruti* over the *smṛti* and the need for new *smṛtis* in response to changing social situations. Obsolete *smṛtis* are what make for stagnation in any religion; and the dominance of the *smṛti* content over its *sruti* content makes for exclusiveness in a religion leading to intolerance, violence, and war. Expounding the traditional view on the subject, Swami Vivekananda says in his lecture on "The Sages of India":

Two ideals of truth are in our scriptures; the one is what we call the eternal, and the other is not so authoritative, yet binding under particular circumstances, times, and places. The eternal relations which deal with the nature of the soul, and of God, and the relations between souls and God are embodied in what we call the *srutis*, the Vedas. The next set of truths is what we call the *smṛtis* as embodied in the works of Manu, Yajnavalkya, and other writers, and also in the Purānas down to the Tantras.

Another peculiarity is that these *srutis* have many sages as the recorders of the truths in them, mostly men, even some women. Very little is known of their personalities, the dates of their birth, and so forth, but their best thoughts, their best discoveries, I should say, are preserved there, embodied in the sacred literature of our country, the Vedas. In the *smṛtis*, on the other hand, personalities are more in evidence. Startling, gigantic, impressive, world-moving persons stand before us, as it were, for the first time, sometimes of more magnitude even than their teachings.

This is a peculiarity which we have to understand, that our religion teaches an impersonal-personal God. It preaches any amount of impersonal laws plus any amount of personality; but the very fountainhead of our religion is in the *srutis*, the Vedas, which are perfectly impersonal; the persons all come in the *smṛtis* and Purānas, the great *avatāras* [incarnations of God], prophets, and so forth. . . . Our religion is not based on persons but principles. That you obey your religion is not because it came through the authority of a sage, no, not even of an incarnation. Krishna is not the authority of the Vedas, but the Vedas are the authority of Krishna himself. His glory is that he is the greatest preacher of the Vedas that ever existed. So with the other incarnations; so with all our sages.

This wisdom of the Indian spiritual tradition finds responsive echoes in several thinkers in the modern age. Says the mathematician-philosopher A. N. Whitehead in *Science in the Modern World:*

> Religion will not regain its old power until it can face change in the same spirit as does science. Its principles may be eternal, but the expression of those principles requires continual development.

Elaborating this truth, historian Arnold Toynbee writes in *An Historian's Approach to Religion:*

> Thus, in our society in our time the task of winnowing the chaff away from the grain in mankind's religious heritage is being forced upon us by a conjunction of social and spiritual circumstances. In the life of all higher religions, the task of winnowing is a perennial one because their historic harvest is not pure grain. In the heritage of each of the higher religions, we are aware of the presence of two kinds of ingredients. There are essential counsels and truths, and there are nonessential practices and propositions. The essential counsels and truths are valid at all times and places, as far as we can see through the dark glass of mankind's experience up to date. . . . But at the same time these same higher religions are historical institutions; and they have been making a transit through space-time in which, at every point-moment in their trajectory, they have been encountering the local and temporary circumstances of human life. . . . These accidental accretions are the price that the permanently and universally valid essence of a higher religion has to pay for communicating its message to the members of a particular society in a particular stage of this society's history.

True religion thus is eternal and universal, but its socio-political expression in the existing world religions is conditioned and limited by historical and cultural factors. The dominance of the latter, reinforced by poor communication facilities arising from technological limitations, explains the social exclusiveness, with its concealed hatred and violence, as in Hinduism, and credal exclusiveness, with its perpetual intolerance and occasional violence, as in several other religions.

Modern physical and mental communication facilities created by technology and the rational spirit engendered by science have rendered the exclusive attitudes of religions an anachronism, and their continuance a sure way to the elimination of religion itself as a creative force in human life. That this recognition has come to the world religions is evidenced by the vast amount of inter-religious dialogue that has taken place during the past decade or two.

This is in tune with the spirit and approach of Hinduism (including the other religions of Indian origin), which among the world's religions, has not only practiced toleration on the largest scale, and this not only by its saints and sages but also by its common people and the political state, but also derives such practice from a rational philosophy. In the words of Dr. S. Radhakrishnan in *Eastern Religions and Western Thought*:

> The Hindu view is not motivated by any considerations of political expediency. It is bound up with its religion and not its policy. . . . The Hindu attitude is based on a definite philosophy. . . . Toleration is the homage which the finite mind pays to the inexhaustibility of the Infinite.

The concept of man upheld in Hinduism is the most vital source of its sanctions for peace. The discovery, by the sages of the Upanishads, of the true nature of man as the *Ātman*, the immortal divine self, and its unity with Brahman, the infinite self of all beings, constitutes the greatest single source of the universality and humanism of Hinduism and its perennial sanction for peace. In advocating further that the object of human life is the steady realization, through life's effort and struggles, of this ever-present truth, that many are the paths that lead to such realization, and that fellowship and harmony should be the watchword among people wending

their way to the same goal through different paths, and that
the secular and the sacred are but the earlier and later phases
of this struggle and realization, Hinduism provides a body of
spiritual insights, tested and verified by sages, saints, and
statesmen in the past, and by Shri Ramakrishna, Swami Vivekananda, and Mahatma Gandhi in the present, capable of
taking modern man on the creative path of fellowship and
peace leading to total life fulfillment.

Man can be viewed from the outside or from the inside.
The former view yields the concept of man as a self-centred,
self-sufficient individual or as a member of a group—social,
political, or religious—endowed with ethical sense and social
awareness limited to the group. When so viewed, it is difficult to overcome the feeling of separateness which is the
source of hatred and violence. Such individuals or such groups
meet each other more often as colliding units than as cooperating entities. Love, cooperation, and service are the
fruits of a spiritual feeling of nonseparateness, a sense of oneness. The view of man from the inside, in his depth, reveals
him in his infinite spiritual dimension which transcends the
limitations of caste or creed, nationality or sex. This is the
central message of Hinduism. This vision of spiritual unity
behind the physical, intellectual, and social diversities is what
helps man to avoid the pitfalls of sectarianism even while belonging to a sect—religious, social, or political. Paul Deussen
has observed that the exhortation of the New Testament to
love your neighbor as yourself is fulfilled only in the vedantic
teaching that you and your neighbor are spiritually one.

This message finds eloquent expression in the sixth and
seventh verses of the Īśā Upanishad which has inspired Hindu
devotees of the past and still inspires millions in the present:

> Whoever sees all beings in his own Self and himself in all
> beings does not, by virtue of that realization, hate any
> one. . . . When, to that knowing sage, all beings are realized
> as existing in his own Self, then what delusion, what sorrow

can afflict him, perceiving as he does the [spiritual] unity [of all existence]?

God is conceived in Hinduism as the *antaryamin,* the inner ruler, of all beings. The Brahadāraṇyaka Upanishad, while developing its majestic exposition of this theme, says:

He who exists in all beings, Who is the innermost truth in all beings, Whom all beings do not know, Whose body are all beings, Who controls all beings from within, This is your Self, the inner Ruler, the Immortal.

In a series of remarkable verses in which God speaks to man, the Srimad Bhagavatam expounds the way of a devotee of God as the way of love and service of all:

I ever abide in all beings as their Self; if man forsakes Me in them and engages himself [exclusively] in worshipping Me in an image, such worship is but folly. Proud men with separatist attitudes who, in hating others, [really] hate Me existing in other beings, and who are filled with such hatred of beings, do not achieve peace of mind. Even if worshipped in an image with elaborate rituals involving accessories big and small, I am not pleased, O Sinless lady, if the worshippers insult the dignity of other beings. Let man, who performs his duties, worship Me in an image, Me Who abide in all beings (as their Self), so long as he is not able to realize Me in his own heart. Therefore worship Me who exist in all beings, who am the Self of all beings, and Who have built My temples in all beings by removing the felt wants of all beings and by upholding their [inborn] dignity, in an attitude of friendliness, and with the eye of nonseparateness. Salute mentally all these beings, showing them due respect, knowing that the blessed Lord [himself] has entered into them as a spark of a soul.

These and innumerable other similar passages in the Hindu scriptures have taught the Hindu essentially to view man, in

himself and in others, in the light of what is inalienable about
him, namely, his innate divine nature, the *Ātman*, and, achieving peace within, project that peace outside in forms of
charity, tolerance, and fellow feeling. Peacelessness and tension
are the characteristics of man as the ego, man at the sensate
level. Hinduism—in fact, every world religion—seeks to take
man above this level and lead him to the experience of the
peace of God. The *Ātman* is described by the Upanishads as
peace. *Shantoyam ātmā* means "this Ātman is peace."

The peace that Hinduism has helped man to mediate outside is the projection of what it has helped him to generate
within himself by the intellectual, moral, and spiritual disciplines that it prescribes for one and all. No spiritual study or
undertaking is commenced without a peace invocation, the
shanti patha. The well-known *shanti patha* of the *Katha* and
some other Upanishads breathe this spirit of peace and love in
abundance:

> Om! May Brahman [God] protect us both [students and
> teacher]; may Brahman nourish us both; may we both ac-
> quire energy [by this study]; May we both become bright
> and illumined by the study. May we not hate each other.
> Om! Peace, peace, peace.

The war which religion summons man to wage is a war
within each person. It is a war to discipline the forces of
egoism and selfishness, lust and greed. To the extent a man
responds to this inner call, to that extent he will be free from
the tendency to wage war with his brother man outside.
Hinduism prescribes a minimum moral and spiritual discipline
for all people in what Patanjali describes as the *mahāvratas*
(great disciplines):

> Non-killing, truthfulness, non-stealing, continence, and non-
> receiving [of gifts] are called *yama* [self-control]. These,

without considerations of caste [or nationality], place, time, and purpose, are great disciplines of universal importance.

The preamble of UNESCO which proclaims that, since wars begin in the minds of men, it is in the minds of men that the defenses of peace should be built, is fundamentally a religious proposition. If there is not peace within, there cannot be peace without. What Dr. Josiah Oldfield said in a speech in London on the eve of the second World War— that more wars were caused by bad-tempered people seeking to discuss peace propositions than by good-tempered people seeking to discuss war measures—is in tune with the essential Hindu attitude. Disciplined in the tenets of Hinduism and its two sister religions, namely, Buddhism and Jainism, the Indian people have been uniformly a nonaggressive people and have not engaged, even when politically and militarily organized into powerful empires, in any war of aggression outside the confines of India; but her inner weakness often tempted foreign aggressors to invade the land and despoil it of its riches. This ingrained love of peace and nonaggressiveness, confronted by the challenge of repeated foreign invasions, is making for the evolution in modern Hinduism of a clearer and more cogent philosophy of peace in which nonaggressiveness is integrated with all-round strength, gentleness becomes coupled with fearlessness. In fact, this is the characteristic of the true devotee of God as described by Shri Krishna in the Gītā:

He by whom the world is not agitated and who (also) is not agitated by the world, who is liberated from excessive elation, intolerance, fear, and anxiety, such a one is dear to Me.

Gandhiji, who derived his message of truth and nonviolence from his ancestral religion, Hinduism, divests his peace and nonviolence of all weakness and cowardice. In a famous article on "The Doctrine of the Sword," Gandhiji says:

> I do believe that when there is only a choice between coward-ice and violence, I would advise violence. I would rather have India resort to arms in order to defend her honor than that she should in a cowardly manner become or remain a helpless victim to her own dishonor. But I believe that non-violence is infinitely superior to violence, forgiveness more manly than punishment. Nonviolence is the law of our species as violence is the law of the brute. The spirit is dormant in the brute and he knows no law but that of physical might. The dignity of man requires obedience to a higher law, to strength of the spirit. The *rishis* (sages) who discovered the law of nonviolence, in the midst of violence, were greater geniuses than Newton. They were themselves greater war-riors than Wellington. Having themselves known the use of arms, they realized their uselessness and taught a weary world that its salvation lay not through violence but through nonviolence.

This study of Hinduism and peace should end with the words of Swami Vivekananda uttered in the course of his lecture on "The Work Before Us." Speaking in Madras in 1897, he discussed the nature of the gift of India to the rest of the world:

> But the gift of India is the gift of religion and philosophy, and wisdom and spirituality. And religion does not want cohorts to march before its path and clear its way. Wisdom and philosophy do not want to be carried on the floods of blood. Wisdom and philosophy do not march upon bleed-ing human bodies, do not march with violence, but come on the wings of peace and love, and that has always been so. . . . The one characteristic of Indian thought is its silence, its calmness. At the same time the tremendous power that is be-hind it is never expressed by violence. It is always the silent

mesmerism of Indian thought. . . . Like the gentle dew that
falls unseen and unheard, and yet brings into blossom the
fairest of roses, has been the contribution of India to the
thought of the world. Silent, unperceived, yet omnipotent in
its effect, it has revolutionized the thought of the world, yet
nobody knows when it did so.

ISLAM
K. G. Saiyadain

I AM MUCH HONORED to present the nature of the relationship
of Islam to peace. It will not be possible for me to do full
justice to this theme, which is crucial to the survival of men
with dignity. Even if, for many persons in the world of
today, an understanding of the nature of reality and the relation of God and man has ceased to have any significance, it
should be a matter of concern to them, as to all of us, to
promote practical and political accommodation and understanding amongst nations and mobilize all possible sources for
the removal of conflicts and war and for the establishment of
a true climate of peace. What contribution can religion as
such, and the great religions individually, make to this ex-
plosive situation? This obviously involves the question, Has
religion any contribution to make?

In the history of man, so many conflicts and persecutions
have been provoked and so many wars precipitated in the
name of religion that many quite well-meaning persons have
turned away from it and are unwilling to seek its cooperation
in their efforts for peace. I think they are ill-advised in adopt-
ing this attitude. Religion needs to be brought into the picture,
because it still has a strong hold on hundreds of millions of
persons in the world and can provide a dynamic motive force
in transforming their attitudes and behavior—can provide but

need not necessarily do so unless we interpret the role of religion correctly.

In history, great crimes have been committed in the name of religions, directly or indirectly, by those who professed to believe in them and by those who were supposed to be their special custodians. I would venture, however, to make the affirmation that whenever they have done so they were not following or honoring the spirit of their religions but were sinning against the light that was in them. They were either myopic or were playing the unscrupulous game of power and exploitation and abusing religion to achieve their unholy purposes. When I speak of Islam and its contribution to peace—as others will speak of the contribution of Hinduism, Christianity, Sikhism, or Jainism—I am not speaking of what many Muslims may have done, and I am not offering any defense of misguided or irreligious Muslim rulers or others who may have strayed away from the path and defied Islam's insistence on peace as the only right way of life. While we should condemn unreservedly persons who have fallen from grace— whatever their religious labels—it would be unfair to place the responsibility for their ungodly and inhuman acts on their respective religions. In judging a religion, we should do so as it is at its best and in the context of its genuine teachings, for what matters in the global context are the elements of rationality, decency, peace, and liberality of mind enshrined in a religion and not all the faults that one can always find in its individual followers. I have considered it necessary to clear away at the outset some sources of misunderstanding which might possibly cloud the discussion, perhaps not in this gathering, but certainly amongst those who do not approach the problem from our angle.

What about Islam's special attitude to the problem of peace and war? What contribution can it make to the situation which confronts us today? Let me make it clear at the outset that Islam is not a pacifist religion in the sense that, under all circumstances and provocations, it prohibits war. Does any religion? But, even in the old days, when wars could in a sense be called almost civilized and often consisted of individual challenges or small group clashes, Islam laid down stringent conditions to control them. A Muslim is never allowed to initiate a war; he can only fight in self-defense or to defend his freedom of belief and worship. The Koran says:

> Fight those who are fighting with you [in order to deprive you of your liberty of conscience] but do not commit any excesses. Allah does not love those who do so.

Even in the heat and the emotional tension of war, the Muslims are enjoined never to deny the enemy water or food or to corrupt their sources of sustenance or to commit any excesses on women and children or the wounded or noncombatant civilian population. The Koran further enjoins:

> Even when you are caught up in a defensive war, if the enemy shows the slightest inclination to peace, respond to it in the fullest measure. If they play you false later, God will look after you.

This means that even the fear of possible treachery on the part of your opponents should not stand in the way of peace negotiations, for the risk of trust is certainly better to take than the risk of suspicion.

What, one may ask, is Islam's basic attitude to the problem of peace? The word Islam comes from the root, *silm*, which literally means peace; its translation by some western scholars as Mohammedanism (or the religion of Mohammed) is not only a semantic mistake but a basic and substantial mistake. Unlike Christianity, Buddhism, or Jainism, Islam is not named after its founder, but after its central purpose which is the promotion of peace and good fellowship in the world. It seeks to bring about peaceful understanding between various

religions, races, colors, tribes, and communities. It views
religion as a continuous, cultural tradition of man and believes
that prophets and reformers have come from God to every
single community and the duty of a Muslim is to honor all
the prophets equally. In the words of the Koran: "There has
been no community to which God's messengers have not
come [and] Muslims should make no distinctions between
them." The Islamic concept of God is not the god of any
particular race, nation, or community, but of the entire human race and a source of *rahmat* (beneficence) for all. Its
greeting for everyone is: "Peace be upon you," whether one
be Hindu, Muslim, Christian, Buddhist, Parsi, Jew—or atheist
for that matter. In the text of the Koran and the Hadis (i.e.,
the traditions or the sayings of the Prophet) this essential
message is woven like a constantly recurring refrain of a
melody. In love, service, unwillingness to offend, settling of
disputes by amicable discussion, and the promotion of peace
lies the reality of life. They are the objectives of Islam—not
conflict, exploitation, hatred, injustice, and war.

Let a few extracts from Hadis speak for themselves: "All
God's creatures are his family and He is most beloved of God
who does real good to the members of God's family." This
means that those who indulge in the game of killing and
torture can claim no favored place in God's bosom. How well
was the truth of this Hadis reiterated in the declaration of the
U.S. Inter-Religious Conference on Peace (1966) when it
said:

> We urge all to pray with us for clarity of mind, integrity
> of spirit, and a deepening inter-religious fellowship that,
> under God, we may be guided through a night of our own
> making to a day when men shall know and love one another
> as God's children.

Again, the Prophet said, swearing by God three times: "And
by God he is no believer; by God he is no believer; by God

he is no believer, whose neighbor does not live in peace because of his mischief making." And today everyone—however different, however far away—is our neighbor in this wide world because the whole world is our village! Again: "May I tell you what is even better than prayers and fasting and giving alms to the poor? It is reconciling differences and disputes among men. And sowing discord wipes off all virtues." This is an injunction that all individuals and nations today will do well to take to heart: "God fills tl ? heart of him with faith and contentment who, having the power to avenge himself, exercises restraint and toleration."

As with tactful insight, the teaching of Islam tries to knock down one by one the psychological props on which the mentality of hatred and war is built up; it makes a valuable contribution to the climate and cause of peace.

Islam does not do merely this; it also probes into the bigger causes which play their ugly part in the precipitation of modern wars—race, religion, color, and nationality. Islam rejects all these totally and unequivocally and by many of his precepts and examples, the Prophet reinforced this lesson. To a considerable extent, Muslims have in practice followed some of its implications. The first person appointed by the Prophet to the high and much prized office of *muezzin*, the man who called the faithful to prayer five times a day, was a black-as-night Negro named Balal. The white, highborn aristocratic members of the tribe of Quraish (to which, incidentally, the Prophet of Islam himself belonged) were displeased and complained to him. He replied that a righteous, God-fearing Negro was, in his view, superior to the highest born member of the tribe of Quraish. This was a knockout blow to the whole doctrine of race and color superiority, which today is one of the most potent causes of war. He went on to reject also the claim of the nation or the *patrie* to be the arbiter of right and wrong and refused to accept the support of wrongdoing by one's country as either a proof of patriotism or an

act of virtue, which all of us readily do today. The Koran
says in uncompromising and unambiguous words:

> O, Ye who believe, be steadfast in the service of God's truth
> and bear witness for justice and let not hatred of a people
> seduce you so that you deal with them unjustly. Act justly
> for that is what piety demands.

The Prophet reinforced this command by adding: "He
who supports a tyrant or oppressor knowing that he is tyrant,
casts himself outside the pale of Islam." Again and again we
find that, in great Islamic literature starting from the Koran
and the Hadis of the Prophet, right through the best of its
poetry, philosophy, and mysticism, a Muslim is often defined
not in narrow theological, doctrinal terms as one who has
recited some prescribed *mantra* and thus become a Muslim,
but with reference to his basic attitudes towards the great
issues that matter in the life of man—war and peace, relationships of groups and individuals, honesty in political and business dealings, and the openness of the heart and mind. This
has to be appreciated not only by followers of other religions,
but also by the Muslims themselves, most of whom are becoming narrow-minded in the interpretation of their religion.

There have been narrow-minded, narrow-hearted, orthodox
interpreters of all religions who have, in their myopic preoc-
cupation with the letter that freezes, missed the spirit that
frees. But they do not present the true face of Islam. This is
the dilemma that not only Islam but every religion faces in
the contemporary world. Will Islam, will the other religions
petrify into rigid dogmas and remain mainly or exclusively
preoccupied with their traditional business of saving the individual soul or will they grow into dynamic movements,
throwing away the flotsam and jetsam from their surface and
respond to the new constructive and destructive forces in
their world? Will they, for instance, be able to meet the chal-

lenge of the atom and the atomic war that hangs like a doom over mankind and teach people how to live in this atomic age? Or will they pusillanimously choose what they consider to be the safe path—that which is in reality the path of the greatest danger—one that sidetracks the most vital and heartbreaking political problems of the day? It is always possible to find refuge in a scriptural sanctuary, but it is neither an act of faith nor of courage to do so. Will Islam reaffirm courageously, without any hesitation or equivocation, its crucial conception of the "universal man" which is the only valid one for this age—the concept of man endowed with the spirit of universal humanism, who makes no distinctions between his personal, his community, and his national good and the good of all mankind and who strives for it with compassion and a sense of righteous indignation?

I have spoken of the permissibility of war in Islam under special circumstances and tried to explain the stringent conditions under which it may be carried on. War today is something radically different from what it was 1,500 or 1,000 or even twenty years ago. Modern war is a technological, nuclear, poison gas, germ war which is calculated to torture and annihilate the human race, to poison the healthy sources of life, including food and water, to maim the unborn child in the mother's womb physically and psychologically, to abolish the frontiers between the combatants and noncombatants, and to wipe out the gracious fruits of man's precious cultural heritage. It cannot obviously be carried on within the kind of conditions envisioned by Islam. There neither is, nor can be, any justification or permission under any religion for participation, directly or indirectly, in such a total war, and I would venture to suggest that every humane, socially sensitive religion should have the courage at least to declare that whoever does participate in such a war is outside its pale. In no religion, no ethics, no code of common sense—in nothing, in fact, except in sheer madness and power lust—can we find the slightest justification for such wars. "Show compassion to those on earth, so that He who is in heaven may show His mercy to you." These identical words were used by Jesus Christ and Prophet Mohammed and one fails to see how compassion can be shown by the use of nuclear bombs or of poison gas and disease germs, which are becoming an essential part of modern warfare.

According to the faith of Islam—and I am sure one could claim the same about other religions because it is part of the highest common ethical legacy of mankind—only good can conquer evil, only love can conquer force. Evil and force can never do so because, in their interaction, they set up a chain reaction of hatred and injustice which never ends. Religions must strike a vigorous blow in that fight for freedom which has been going on in the world since the dawn of history—a blow to shatter the chains which bind man's spirit in the name of race and religion, geography and nationalism, caste and color. The real fight of the future is not so much against the forces of nature which man has won or is well on the way to winning. It is rather man's fight against his own nature—its meanness, its cruelty, its desire to exploit others, and its denial of justice to his fellow men. It is against his own narrowness and stupidity which persist in spite of the great advances in his knowledge. It is against the twisted complexes that snarl inside him and give him no peace, within or without. The best contribution that Islam can make to the world is to assist in the process of the emergence of the new man who will be able to define his priorities more intelligently and compassionately and live by these priorities, who will welcome technology but not barter his soul in the process, who will be more concerned with giving than with taking, and who will strive for peace with every resource of his being.

In a message which President Johnson sent to the National Inter-Religious Conference on Peace at Washington in 1966, he said:

The billions we appropriate to conquer poverty will be worth little unless we vanquish the most crippling poverty—man's insufficiency of understanding, his meagreness of spirit. The dollars we spend to eradicate disease will be wasted unless we isolate and control the deadliest of microbes—man's capacity for hatred, his penchant for violence. Living in such a world has taught us that our only victories will be won, not by putting more weapons in men's hands but by putting more wisdom in their hearts.

All that one asks of President Johnson, and of a few other men in positions similar to his, is that they live up to their own professions! Then alone will they be able to respond to the message and the spirit of religion and lead the world out of the darkening gloom. Otherwise the mere mouthing of pious phrases, whether by the highest and the mightiest or by all men and women in the world put together, cannot bring peace any nearer.

ZOROASTRIANISM

Dastoor N. D. Minochehr-Homji

> Whoever wins, on that side shall I lose;
> Assured loss before the match be played.
> —*King John*, Act III, Sc. i. ll. 35–36

IF THIS is the political predicament in which we live, it is incumbent upon us all to learn some useful lessons from religion so as to live in peace with all.

Zoroastrianism defines peace (*akshti*) as the product of fellow-feeling (*hamvainti*), and the latter comes by the acknowledgement of the unity of mankind. As Saadi, the Persian poet (1184–1291), the celebrated author of *Gulestan* (1258), has put it:

The races of man are but the limbs of one another,
Who in their creation spring from the one essence:
When one member of the body is eventually afflicted,
The rest of the members are never at rest.

Besides the acknowledgement of the unity of man, there must be personal conviction that right makes might (as Abraham Lincoln put it) or there must be harmony in the family to have order in the nation and that will give, ultimately, peace in the world. We quote the beautiful Chinese proverb:

If there is righteousness in the heart, there will be beauty in the character. If there is beauty in the character, there will be harmony in the home. If there is harmony in the home, there will be order in the nation. If there is order in the nation, there will be peace in the world.

The ancient Zoroastrians valued peace between the nations far above other types. *Mithra*, the universal cementing principle of love between individuals as between groups and nations is obtaining

twenty-fold between two friends or two relations;
thirty-fold between two men of the same group (or guild);
forty-fold between two partners;
fifty-fold between wife and husband;
sixty-fold between two pupils (of the same master);
seventy-fold between the pupil and his master;
eighty-fold between the son-in-law and his father-in-law;
ninety-fold between two brothers;
a hundred-fold between the father and the son;
a thousand-fold between two nations;
ten thousand-fold when connected with the Law of Mazda;
and then he will be every day of victorious strength.

—Sacred Books of the East, Vol. 23, p. 149.

Darmesteter, the French savant, has an illuminating note on the above:

> Or, "the contract is twenty-fold . . ." that is, twenty times more strictly binding than between any two strangers. This passage is one of the most important of the Avesta, as a short account of the social constitution and morals of Zoroastrian Iran.

Quite the reverse picture is drawn regarding the sad plight of the world, because of the unsocial and antisocial, therefore inhuman, behavior of men of different types prevalent in the world. Let us check and try to remove these types from amongst us:

> We worship the Fravashis of the Virtuous to withstand the wrong done by (i) *oppressors*, misappropriating the power and authority; to withstand the wrong done by (ii) *the brigand*, the exploiter, the hoarder; to withstand the wrong done by (iii) *the dead-in-conscience*, oblivious to the social good; and to withstand the wrong done by (iv) *those yielding to passion-and-wrath-and-violence*.
>
> —Yasht. 13, 135–38: *SBE*, Vol. 23, pp. 223–24.

The last reference to passion-wrath-violence leads us to Zarathustra's indictment of the same. The world has suffered from the same untold harm in all lands, in all periods of history. Zarathustra sings in his message in the Gathas (songs):

> Hatred shall be kept down, steel yourselves against violence, [all ye] who wish-to-hold-fast-on-to Vohu Man [the ways of wisdom-virtue-love].
>
> —Dr. Taraporevala: The Gathas. Yasna,
> 48, 7: cp. *SBE*, Vol. 31, pp. 156–57.

When the ruling passion is passion to rule, the physically weaker but morally good individual or the nation suffers unjustifiably, for "might is right" is the order of the day, and Zoroastrian scripture delineates the faithful picture:

> When the meek in spirit, who follows the good Law, when wronged and deprived of his rights, invokes Mithra, the spirit of Justice, for help, with hands uplifted.
>
> —Yasna, 10, 84: *SBE*, Vol. 23, p. 140.

But even when we have to encounter hatred and violence, Zarathustra, the Bactrian sage, advises persuasion, which is the result of inner strength.

The remedy, as we have seen in the Chinese proverb, lies in righteousness, as the prevailing order among men. Zarathustra has come in an age of inner darkness and outer violence, and took the pledge:

> As long as I have will and am physically capable,
> So long will I teach mankind
> To strive for truth-order-and-harmony.
>
> —Yasna, 28, 4: *SBE*, Vol. 31, pp. 19–20.

Then we see this warning:

> Never for a second time shall the False teacher
> Distort the scheme of values
> And thus poison the stream of life.
>
> —Yasna, 45, 1: *SBE*, Vol. 31, p. 125.

Let us end with a Zoroastrian prayer that enumerates some six values that can make life worthwhile:

> May (i) *Sroasha* (willing obedience to meaningful injunctions of life) conquer disobedience within this house, and may (ii) peace triumph over discord here, and (iii) generous giving over avarice, (iv) reverence over contempt, (v) speech with truthful words over lying utterance. May (vi) the Righteous Order gain the victory over the Lie.
>
> —Yasna, 60, 5: *SBE*, Vol. 31, p. 311.

JUDAISM

Rabbi Maurice N. Eisendrath

IT IS MOST APPROPRIATE that this Symposium on religion and peace should take place in this ancient land of India. Not alone has India's recent history provided an inspiration and challenge to the Western world's faith in force by virtue of its Gandhian confidence in the force of faith, but long before Gandhi and his demonstration of the power of the spirit, the religious thrust of this nation manifested a rare hospitality to all forms of religious expression. As was emphasized by Earnest Benz, in an address honoring former President S. Radhakrishnan:

> The conception of religion, as deeply rooted in Hinduism, sees in all religions of history only the outward form, the revelations and manifestations of the one transcendental God, who has revealed himself in different ways to different nations and communities at different times and in different places. Krishna, the sublime, says to Arjuna in the Bhagavat-gītā, "There is no end to my glorious manifestation. Behold, therefore, my forms, hundred and thousandfold, manifold, divine, various in color and shape—behold many miracles such as have never before been seen." It was as true heir of such breadth of vision that Radhakrishnan himself insisted that "If the great religions continue to waste their energies in fratricidal struggle, instead of regarding themselves as friendly partners in the supreme task of fostering the spiritual life of mankind, then no further obstacle will stand in the way of the rapid advance of moral materialism."

It is in consonance with this spirit of mutual respect and respective appreciation that I would now explore those sanctions in my own more than five-thousand-year-old Jewish faith, Judaism, which constrain me to join with you in pursuing this golden goal of peace which my Jewish forbears designated as "God's most precious gift." It must be confessed from the outset, however, that Judaism is not predicated upon absolute pacifism. The ideal of universal peace is envisaged in that sublime vision of Isaiah: "Swords beaten into ploughshares and spears into pruning hooks, of nation no longer making war against nation, of every man sitting 'neath his own vine and fig tree, there being none to make him afraid." Though this vision and this aspiration comprise one of the most exalted aims of Western religion, nevertheless this ideal of peace has been rudely shattered by not a few realistic trials by physical force which have pervaded my Hebraic past. My distant progenitors were not unqualified pacifists. They did not believe in peace at any price. As with other nations of the time, Israel was all too frequently rocked by war and strife. And its people responded in kind. The sensitive prophet cried out: "Not by might and not by power, but by My spirit, saith the Lord." But the people of Israel ofttimes did march forth to battle—and not invariably in self-defense. They even proclaimed that they fought in God's name "the battles of the Lord." They battled in His name and for His glory. It was only after the utter destruction of their state in the year 70 C.E., that this haunting vision of universal peace became incorporated in the "mission of Israel."

As George Holley Gilbert points out in *The Bible and Universal Peace:*

> The ancient Hebrews had a warlike career. They fought the battles of Yahweh for centuries. But when at last their national existence was no more, when they sat and sighed by the ruins of their holy city, or far away among the nations, some among them dreamed of a new and wondrous age that was yet to come. They thought of their past, glorified, indeed, in the far retrospect. But they did not long to have those ages returned unchanged. They dreamed of a future

that should be far better than the best that their fathers had ever known. And one constant element of that great future —one on which they dwelt with satisfaction—was peace. Out of the soul of centuries of strife and bloodshed blossomed, as a fair lover, the vision of a time when peace should flow as a river. By this vision the Hebrew prophets became leaders of the race toward a future kingdom whose realization is still among the treasures of hope.

From that day forward, it was the intellectual and spiritual academy, established by Rabbi Jochanon ben Zakkai, rather than the military resistance of the Zealots, that enabled the Jew to survive so resounding a political debacle. The contribution of Israel and of its faith, Judaism, was not only its vision, its dream, its preachment of peace, its ideal of peace, at a time when war was still the standard state of affairs and the normal affair of states. It was also the extraordinary commitment to the pursuit of peace for all nations. In an age when these nations were divided by gulfs seldom crossed except by military forces, the prophecies of Amos and Micah sent forth shafts of light which, like the beams of stars that reach the earth after eons of time, are only now beginning to illumine the earth. As a matter of fact, the rabbinic commentators on the Bible specifically pointed out that the injunction not only to "love peace" but to "pursue peace" was the one Biblical behest which explicitly enjoined an active and passionate pursuit of its realization. Thus, the rabbis of the Midrash insisted that:

> The Torah does not command you to run after or to pursue the other commandments, but only to fulfill them upon the appropriate occasion. But peace you must seek in your own place and pursue it even to another place as well.

Even before this metamorphosis, imposed by the destruction of its own, its native land and its agelong exile from the sacred soil of the Promised Land, while the kings of Israel and their obedient subjects fought for home and motherland, opposition to war was heard loud and frequently within Israel's frontiers. The prophet Jeremiah, even with the hordes of Babylon hammering at the very gates of Jerusalem, vigorously and vocally opposed the taking up of arms on the part of king and countrymen against the adversary. Standing alone against the Establishment of his day, he denounced even self-defensive resistance and urged his people to submit rather than to be destroyed. True he was regarded as a traitor, imprisoned and all but executed. But the subsequent inclusion of Jeremiah's bitter denunciation of his nation's policy within the canon of the Hebrew scripture is a clear indication that, not only the hope for peace, but the active opposition to war, in the most direct and concrete fashion possible, became a real and authentic option in Judaism. Isaiah, too, denounced his people's futile and dangerous military alliances and warned against the tragic consequences which they would incur. There is likewise that little known episode in the Hebrew Bible of the Prophet confronting the victorious armies of Israel, marching triumphantly with thousands of Judean captives, and demanding that they be returned. There is also the incident of Elisha who insisted that the king of Israel release the enemies whom God had led into his hand. And what of the interdiction against David fulfilling his fondest aspiration to build the temple in his newly captured city of Jerusalem because, as a man of war, his hands were stained with blood— an interdiction, by the way, which was subsequently embodied into actual talmudic law, as expressed in the restriction against selling iron to idol worshipers lest they convert it into weapons of battle.

Just as Gandhi, in our day, took certain warlike sections in the Bhagavadgītā and reinterpreted them saying that "the conflict is between right and wrong, and human personality is the battleground," so the rabbis allegorized and spiritualized most biblical portrayals of violence. Where the Bible speaks of Abraham's leading forth his "trained men," a talmudic comment has it that these were not warriors but "scholars of the law." With reference to that which Jacob once took from the Amorites with sword and bow, the exegesis is that "sword" means prayer and "bow" means supplication. Joshua, though causing the walls of Jericho to collapse, is transmuted into a man of peace. David, the builder of an empire, is honored for his Psalms, not his military victories. In general, it is pointed out, whenever there is mention of "heroes," it should be taken to signify "heroes of Torah," as is said in one of the Psalms! "Ye heroes of strength that fulfill the word of the Lord." In the *Ethics of the Fathers*, a hero is one who masters his passions, in the *Ethics* of R. Nathan, it is added, "the supreme hero is he who converts a foe into a friend."

It is remarkable, too, that throughout the traditional Jewish calendar and liturgy, with their myriad recollections, there is no conscious commemoration of any event (or at least that aspect of it) in which Israelites themselves had shed blood, such as the rout of the Amalekites, the conquest of Canaan, the wars of the Judges and Kings, or the Hyrcanus conversion of the Idumeans. One exception perhaps is Purim. Yet, here, too, in the popular consciousness, the fast of Esther loomed far more significant than the defense of Shushan.

According to all phases of Judaism, there is one attribute of God to be emulated above all others—the attribute of compassion. "As He is merciful, be ye merciful." And there is one principle of Torah which towers over all the rest: love of neighbor as oneself. This must be so, once all men are seen as kin and each person of enduring worth.

Though in its own tribal origins, Israel was not untainted by the blood of military conflict, nevertheless the belief in the all-conquering power of love, and in the invincible strength of the spirit were not exclusive characteristics of other faiths, supplanting the alleged "God of vengeance." How can any

serious student of the Hebrew Bible dismiss what was tanta-
mount to the ensuing Christian gospel of "turning the other
cheek," to be discerned, not only in the teaching, but in the
exemplary life of the compassionate prophet, Hosea? Surely
he took far more punishment from his wayward, insolently
adulterous wife, Gomer, than the mere turning of the other
cheek. Likewise a later rabbinic legend portrays God as
chastising the angels of heaven who wanted to exalt Him in
ecstatic hymns of thanksgiving when the waves of the Red
Sea closed over the drowning Egyptians: "My creatures are
perishing and you want to sing praises." This has a striking
relevance to the rejoicing, on the part of too many of our
contemporaries, over the reports of North Vietnamese peas-
ants struck down, not by the waves of the Red Sea, but by the
waves of American bombing planes and scorching napalm.
And what of the far more explicit admonition of the Book of
Proverbs which so categorically commands: "If thine enemy
be hungry, give him bread to eat, and if he be thirsty, give
him water to drink." This called forth the even more specific
behest of the rabbis enjoining: "If thine enemy rise up early
and come to thine house to slay thee, if he be hungry, give
him bread to eat and if he be thirsty, give him water to
drink." "It is good that a man bear the yoke in his youth,"
wrote the author of Lamentations, "Let him put his mouth in
the dust; if so be there may be hope." And then the striking
pre-Christian—and pre-Gandhian also—injunction: "Let him
give his cheek to him that smiteth him. Let him be filled with
shame."

"In every other law of the Torah," we read in the Talmud,
"if a man is commanded, 'Transgress and suffer not death,' he
may transgress and not suffer death excepting idolatry, incest,
and shedding blood. Murder may not be practiced to save
one's life." Long before the Nuremberg trials and Eichmann,
long before the latter-day groping toward the concept of the
inviolate right of conscience and of individual responsibility,

those rabbis of the early centuries of the common era unambiguously recounted this specific example:

> Even as one who came before Raba and said to him, "The governor of my town has ordered me 'Go and kill so and so; if not, I will slay thee.'" Raba answered him "Let him rather slay you than that you should commit murder. Who knows that your blood is redder? Perhaps his blood is redder than yours!"

Small wonder, then, that the rabbis extolled peace virtually above all other ideals, that "peace be unto you" became the centuries-old greeting of the Jew in obedience to the rabbinic behest to "intone the blessing of peace in entering, to intone it in departing as well." They also maintained that "great is peace for it weighs as much as all else in the world." Amazing was their further insistence that "even if Israel stumbles into idolatry, but yet maintains peace, God will not permit Satan to touch them." Amazing in very truth is this assertion on the part of teachers who sought to "build a fence around the Torah" in order to protect the children of Israel from any chance contact with the pagan idolaters that surrounded them and who burned at the stake rather than deny the living God, and yet had the audacity to assert that, even if the Jews assimilated themselves to such forbidden practices, God would not permit Satan to touch them. Still further, these rabbinic commentators voiced their apotheosis of peace as the most exalted goal of all, for "great is peace," they averred, "because even in times of war, it is incumbent to proclaim peace. Great is peace," they concluded, "because the very name of God is called 'Shalom.'"

These are not mere isolated proof texts. They are but illustrations undergirding the very theology from which they arose, a theology which insisted that all aspects of reality and experience must be attributed to a single God, to an all-encompassing unity as affirmed in "Hear, O Israel, the Lord, our God, the Lord is one." This is a theology, transmitted through ritual and rite, liturgy and literature, folkways and festivals, all of which—yes, even the Maccabean feast exalting the rededication of the temple rather than the military victory —labeled the exultation of violence and the absence of compassion and even killing in sport as woefully, blasphemously un-Jewish.

Dr. Steven S. Schwarzchild has written:

> God, to the Jew, is the radical of radicals, the 'Ikkar ha 'Ikkarim, the root of all roots! As Karl Marx reminds us in a famous passage, to be radical means to go to the root. Marx went on to claim that the root of man is man. Judaism, however, insists that the root of man is God. Consequently, when God, the radical, the root of all roots, demands that we seek peace, He demands radically that we radically seek radical peace. Hence, when He demands, "Seek peace and pursue it," He did not mean seek war, nor did He mean seek peace when it is prudent, popular, or conducive to one's own selfish or national interest. Nor yet did He mean seek peace slowly, under certain and not under other conditions. Because the God of the religious Jew is the root of all radicalism, He is bound to be radical in every respect, insisting on peace now and everywhere—in the methods of operation as well as with respect to the Goal.

The distinction between "offensive" and "defensive" wars is, of course, a very old one in Christendom. Judaism, however, makes a different fundamental distinction between "commanded" and "permitted" wars. "Commanded" wars were those which the Bible describes as divinely ordered against "the seven original Palestinian peoples and the Amalekites." But this very law placed it in the closed chapters of the past without any possible bearing upon the present. Since these nations no longer exist, such commanded wars are no longer conceivable. Just the same, even retroactively, the great medieval Jewish philosopher, Maimonides, attenuated the commandment of "obligatory" wars by permitting them only if the enemy had explicitly refused to accept the duties of the minimal moral law incumbent upon all human beings. As for "permitted" wars, that is, wars to be determined by human considerations, they might be entered into only with the specific permission of the great Sanhedrin of 71 members. Thus, at least for Jewish purposes, this category of war has also become but a memory, inasmuch as the Sanhedrin long since came to an end and realistically is all but unreconstitutable.

Far from being any mere theoretical value stance, this pursuit of peace was incorporated into the very codes of law by which the life of the Jew, down to every slightest, most infinitesimal detail was regulated. The book of Deuteronomy, even though distinguishing between "commanded" and "permitted" wars, severely restricts most accepted rules of warfare, such as "sparing all women and children, fruit trees, and water supplies," exempting "the newly married" and sending back from the battlefront, not only all those who declare their scruples against bearing arms, but even those who confess that "they are afraid." Today, who is not afraid of the big, bad bomb? "When in your war against a city," Deuteronomy admonishes, "you have to besiege it a long time. You must not destroy its trees, wielding an axe against them. You may eat of them, but you must not cut them down." What a glaring contrast to our complacent acceptance of scorched earth! And how contemporaneous is Maimonides when in his *Treatise on Kings and Wars* he writes:

> When siege is laid to a city for the purpose of capture, it may not be surrounded on four sides, but only on three in order to give an opportunity for escape to those who would flee to save their lives.

This is a far cry, indeed, from our contemporary craving for complete capitulation, for unconditional surrender, for the tactics of "hot pursuit" no matter what frontiers of sovereign states are violated in the process.

But the realism of the Jew went still further in its striving to abolish war and all its multitudinous evils. Realistic as normative Judaism ever strove to be, it sought to ferret out the causes of war, rather than merely to restrict it when it broke out. And foremost among the causes of war, even in those distant days, thousands of years ago, was poverty, want, hunger—that same hunger and want which sent the first hunters foraging for food and pillaging the flocks and herds of their neighbors. Thus it is more than mere accident or a titillating play on words which finds in the Hebrew appellation for "war" a far more meaningful connotation than in its English counterpart, the French *la guerre*, the Latin *bellum*, or any similar term in the lexicon of most other peoples. The Hebrew word for war is *milchomoh*, which is directly derived from the verb *locham*, which intriguingly enough means both to "feed" as well as to "wage war." It was this identification of the search, the need for food and the call to battle, which impelled the Jewish sages to assert: "It is for want of adequate provisions that men are tempted to fare forth to war." This is an ancient diagnosis of a still all too contemporaneous cause of international conflict. A categoric sanction of Judaism to "feed the hungry, to clothe the naked, and to take the homeless into thy habitation" is the most formidable antidote to war.

Such is the sanction of Judaism for universal, all-inclusive peace, predicated, of course, upon its indomitable faith in the oneness of God and the all-inclusive oneness of His children, of all peoples, races, and faiths of man. Our contemporary society and our respective national states, the state of Israel included, seem not yet completely capable of complying with this divine dictum. Most of us have drifted much too far from the worship of and obedience to the "one God," from the father of us all which most of us profess, to anticipate any mass conversion from our idolization of Mars and Mammon, all too characteristic of our yet henotheistic generation. *Realpolitik* is in truth the order of the day for all our nation-states, great and small. This is true for the state of Israel as well, which reluctantly, and regretfully, found itself manning the barricades against the politicide which once again, as in ages past, threatened its existence and the annihilation of its citizens. Even in the face of a military victory, more phenomenal than any annals of the past recount, there was a sobriety which contrasted mightily with what might have been the warranted trumpeting of triumph.

While there is danger in the land of Israel, even as in every other political or national entity, of a newborn chauvinism—as in India when the borders of Tibet or Kashmir clash with the behests of Buddha, or in the United States when Christian teaching is vitiated by so-called national interests in Vietnam —so there is danger in Israel of an adulation of the idol of the state, so altogether antithetical to the whole thrust of Jewish theology and destiny. I do believe that whatever may be the pragmatic compulsions of the state struggling for survival today, or at any rate tomorrow, as in the besieged Jerusalem of Jeremiah and Isaiah of yesterday, there will yet be heard the ancient echoes of that faith in the spirit, which is the treasured gift of Judaism, by the Western world at least. That heritage was expressed in our own time by the late Martin Buber who, as a citizen of contemporary Israel, still echoed the accents of his ancient prophetic past in stating:

> In the closed sphere of the exclusively political, there is no way to penetrate the factual life of factual men nor to relieve—the existential mistrust which divides the world into hostile camps—the present situation whose "natural end" is the technically perfect suicide of the entire human race— the solidarity of all separate groups in the flaming battle for the becoming of one humanity is, in the present hour, the highest duty on earth. . . . In every decision we must strug-

gle, with fear and trembling, lest it burden us with greater guilt than we are compelled to assume, with dangerous arrogance, too, if we believed that any individual, any nation, any ideology has a monopoly on rightness, liberty, and human dignity.

Not only in the words of so wise a philosopher, so rare a spirit, as Buber does Judaism's centuries-old passion for peace pulsate still in the soul of the Jew. Even the most tough-minded Israelis, who do not tend to be sentimental and who shrink from any public exhibition of inner feeling, leaned upon the ancient stones of the wailing wall and wept unabashedly, reflecting in its symbolic adumbration of Judaism's abhorrence of war an act unsurpassed in human history, certainly in military chronicles. Similarly Major General Yitzhak Rabin, chief of staff of Israel's defense forces, delivered an address in the amphitheater of the Hebrew University on Mount Scopus unique in the annals of a victorious military commander:

> Rhetorical phrases and clichés are not common in our army, but this scene on the temple mount, beyond the power of words to describe, revealed as though by a flash of lightning, truths that were deeply hidden. This joy of triumph has seized the entire nation. Nevertheless, a strange phenomenon can be observed among our soldiers. Their joy is incomplete, and their celebrations are marred by sorrow and shock. There are even some who abstain from celebrations entirely. The men in the front lines saw with their own eyes not only the glory of victory, but also the price of victory—their comrades fallen beside them soaked in blood. I know too that the terrible price paid by our enemies also touched the hearts of our men. It may be that the Jewish people has never learned and never accustomed itself to feel the triumph of conquest and victory, with the result that these are accepted with mixed feelings.

Thus, the God of our fathers is not dead, nor silent. He thunders still, more insistently than ever, in the selfsame strains which Buber imbibed from his Jewish teaching. This struggle between the Lord and Satan, between the Lord of all and the martial gods of men, between an intrinsically Jewish commitment to peace and the expedient summons of war, is sensitively adumbrated in one of the most haunting volumes of our time, entitled *Dawn*, by that perceptive Jewish author, Elie Wiesel. It tells of a young Jew who survived a Nazi concentration camp, a member of the Irgun extremists who has been ordered by his superiors to execute a British officer as a reprisal. The deed was to take place at dawn. Throughout the interminable night the young man's conscience was tormented. Within him raged a war between the traditional Jewish values and the seemingly ineluctable exigencies of his beleaguered nation. The latter presents its argument as follows:

> We have no other choice. For generations we have wanted to be better, more pure in heart than those who persecuted us. You've all seen the result: Hitler and the extermination camps of Germany. We've had enough of trying to be more just, more peace-loving than those who claim to speak in the name of those virtues. If ever it's a question of killing off Jews, everyone is silent—there are twenty centuries to prove it. The commandment, "Thou shalt not kill," was given from the summit of one of the mountains here in Palestine and we were the only ones to obey it. But that's all over now. We must become like everybody else.

So spoke the contemporary, the tough-minded, brave-hearted native of Israel reborn, whose craving is to have his nation and his people become "like unto all the other peoples" of the earth.

The rejoinder, from traditional Judaism, as lovingly recounted by Wiesel asks: "Where is God to be found—even now, even today? When is a man most truly a man? When he submits or when he refuses? Where does suffering lead him? To purification or to bestiality?" The debate lasts throughout the long night.

It is a debate which persists for decades because it poses the fundamental dilemma of modern Jewish life, of contemporary Israel, of all humanity in this gravest of all hours. This latter-day yearning for normalcy—so called—is understandable. So is the vicarious gratification which millions of Jews have experienced in the miraculous military prowess of Israel. But the question remains: what is the unique contribution which Judaism and the Jew have bequeathed to our generation? To me, it is still subsumed in that glorious summation of "not by might and not by power, but by My spirit shall man [and Israel too, in the long run] prevail." It is to hearken still to that voice, ringing down the ages and challenging us still to strive, though the price be high and the risk grave and the sacrifice great, to wed words to works and prayer to practice—as each Sabbath, in our synagogues, Jews reach the climax of our liturgy in the surging "Song of Peace," eagerly entreating God to

> grant us peace, Thy most precious gift, O Thou eternal source of peace, and enable Israel to be its messenger unto the peoples of this earth. Strengthen the bonds of friendship and fellowship among the inhabitants of all lands. Plant virtue in every soul and may the love of Thy name hallow every heart. Praised be thou, O Lord, our God, giver of peace.

As this is Judaism's "Sanction for Peace," so have we here learned that so many of our sister and daughter faiths have proclaimed similar categoric commands for "Peace on earth to men of good will." Shall we not then, together, we who number so many hundreds of millions, more by far than all the hosts of warmongers in the world combined, mingle our voices with all those maimed and murdered, widowed and orphaned, join hand to hand and heart to heart? Cannot then all this present fratricide, this deicide, this slaughter of God's image in man cease ere we reduce our earth to shambles, so that not only shall "swords and spears," but bombing planes and intercontinental missiles too, "be beaten into ploughshares and pruning hooks"—and tanks into harvesting machines— that "every man indeed sit beneath his vine and fig tree there being none"—neither Viet Cong guerillas nor alien bombers— "to make him afraid"? Then, in the words of Isaiah, there will be "no harm or destruction in all God's holy mountain, for the land shall be full of the knowledge of God as the waters cover the sea."

SIKHISM

Gopal Singh, M.P.

SIKHISM IS NOT, strictly speaking, a system of philosophy, but a way of life. "Truth," said Guru Nanak, "is above everything, but higher by far is the living of truth."

I wonder if there has been a world religion which did not advocate world peace. But how many of them practiced it is a different story. If by wishing peace to the world, you renounce the world, believing it to be false, illusory, or *māyā;* or if you attribute man's origin to sin which can be washed out only through a single door; or if you divide the world into that of the infidel and the faithful, or black and white, the chosen and the condemned, how would you make one believe that you look upon humankind as one, or worthy to be saved except your way—or, being illusory, worthy of being saved at all? Perhaps the highly mystic concepts and terms, like *māyā,* genesis, original sin, heaven and hell, need to be understood in their true context and import, and not literally, as heretofore. A wind of change—very welcome indeed—is blowing through the religious world, as at the Vatican, accepting the validity of religions other than one's own and reinterpreting the inessential in dogma in terms of the essential in life. Our latest religion of peacemongers is world communism wishing to integrate mankind through hatred and class war, and decimation of everything spiritual in man which distinguishes man from the animal. However, a faction —an important faction so far—of these "gentlemen of the fury" has opted (one hopes, for good) for coexistence in spite of the staggering stockpile of their intercontinental missiles.

Sikhism, however, though the youngest of world religions (being barely 500 years old) does not hold truth to be its sole monopoly. Says the third *guru*, Amar Das: "The world is on fire. Save it. O God, save it in Thy mercy through whichever door it cometh to Thee." God is one, but His manifestations are many. "O God, I'm a sacrifice to all the names Thou hast," proclaims Nanak. That is how, in the Sikh scripture, the Guru Granth Sahib, God is venerated through a thousand names. Yet, in the end, it is said, "Not this; not this." Guru Gobind Singh, the tenth and the last Sikh *guru*, called God the "God of no-religion," for if God be identified only with a particular religion, then his grace and mercy are denied to the others. It is for this reason that the Sikh scripture does not merely incorporate the sayings of the Sikh *gurus* but also of the Hindu *bhaktas* and the Muslim *sufis*. The foundation stone of the central Sikh temple of worship, the Hari Mandir in Amritsar, was laid by a Muslim *sufi*, Sain Mian Mir. The *guru* gave this temple four doors, signifying thereby that his religion was open to all the four castes and all the four main religions then current, and to all the four directions. When Guru Nanak proclaimed the essence of his religion, for the first time, the words that he uttered were: "I find in this world neither a Hindu, nor a Muslim; only man." The *guru*, Gobind Singh, proclaimed equally vehemently: "The temple and the mosque are the same: the same are the *pooja* and the *nimaz*. Men are the same all over, though each a different appearance has."

Sikhism, thus, does not divide the world into for and against, not even into good and bad. Says Nanak: "O God, whom shall I call bad, when there is not another without Thee." Man is not born in sin, according to Sikhism, for originating from a pure source called God, how could impurities attach to him, except through voluntary choice, that is to say, howsoever much we are allowed by our heredity, environment, education, and social structure to exercise our freewill. But, all the same, it is how and what we choose that determines our humanity—not what we think or believe or who we are. The world, according to Sikhism, is real, because its creator, our God, is real. How he created is not, according to Sikhism, a fit subject of inquiry; it is there before us to see and deal with. The purpose of the religious is not to merge in the void, or withdraw from its snares, or responsibilities, or to work for the emancipation of the individual soul as distinct from the corporate society, or to work for a release into a heaven in the hereafter. If man's destiny is emancipation, or *mukti*, as Sikhism enjoins, then it must be realized on this very earth, not only for the self, but for the whole society. Says Guru Arjun: "O God, I seek neither dominions, nor emancipation, I crave only the love of Thy feet." And again: "O God, if Thou emancipatest me after death, who will know that Thou are the emancipator of the souls?"

Therefore, it is for living emancipation that a Sikh yearns and works ceaselessly. The test of the awakened one, or the God-conscious being, according to Guru Arjun is: "For the God-conscious, the primary duty is to flow out of himself." The worst malady that afflicts man and separates him from the rest of his kind is "I-amness." According to the Sikh credo, he who is I-conscious cannot be God-conscious. The closing words of the Sikh prayer are: "Blest by Nanak, the *guru,* may our spirits be ever in the ascendency. O God, may the whole world be blessed in Thy will and mercy."

What kind of a world order does Sikhism seek to bring about? Says Guru Arjun: "My compassionate Lord has given the command that no one will give pain to another. And whosoever is, will live in peace: And the poor in spirit will reign supreme."

At another place, he says: "He who has more, is afflicted with care. He who has less craves for more. It is only he who neither has less nor more that is in peace."

Ravidas, whose work is quoted in the Sikh scripture, puts it even more clearly:

> The city of my love is without grief. There, no one paineth another, nor feareth. There's no tax on goods, and no anxiety afflicteth man. And erreth here no one, nor is afraid of another, and compassion is never in want.

Says Guru Nanak: "He who rules over another is a fool, an indiscriminate wretch."

Though the tenth *guru,* like the sixth, his grandfather, had to draw the sword to protect not only his own right but the right of everyone to live according to his own conscience; he still made it clear that the sword was to be used only as the last resort, and employed with no rancor in the heart even against the enemy.

Secular power should be used not to overpower others, but to make the world safe for men of conscience. Writing to Aurangzeb in what is called the "Letter of Victory," *Guru* Gobind Singh clearly pleaded for open diplomacy and a resort to arms only in self-defense, and that, too, when all other avenues had been exhausted. Says he in this letter:

> Do not wield the sword to murder the innocent, for the God on high would for sure punish thee. He who acteth

honestly, him the God saveth to perform His service. So, whatever one's strength, one must annoy not the weak and thus destroy one's roots.

It is a fact of history that *Guru* Tegh Bahadur, the ninth Sikh *guru*, whose shrine stands to his eternal memory in Delhi, courted martyrdom for the protection of a religion not his own. He was in fact accepting the challenge of Aurangzeb on behalf of all men of conscience, all over.

The seventh *guru*, Hari Rai, kept a cavalry of 2,200 with him, but never used it. He would go out hunting, capture birds, but never kill them, and release them once again into freedom. Once, a flower struck by the loose garments of his flowing gown fell off its stem. He was so much filled with remorse that forever thereafter he kept assembled in his arms the folds of his gown. Even though it cost him his head, the fifth *guru*, Arjun, gave asylum to the rebel prince, Khusro, who was fleeing from the tyranny of the emperor, Jehangir, his father. So did the seventh Guru Hari Rai help Dara Shikoh, the elder brother of Aurangzeb, against the onslaught of the emperor. And is it not a miracle of history that Guru Gobind Singh, the tenth *guru*, whose father, four sons, and mother were martyred by Aurangzeb or his viceroy at Sirhind, helped his son, Bahadur Shah, a great liberal and *sufi* of his times, in his battle of succession against his brothers, even if, in the end, the same Bahadur Shah was to put a price on the head of every Sikh?

In the battlefield of Anandpur, a Sikh follower of Guru Gobind Singh, Kanihya by name, was ministering water to the wounded both on his side as well as the enemy's. He was reported to the *guru* for this misdemeanor. Kanihya replied: "When I served water, I did so minding not who was my enemy, or who was my friend, for I saw no one other than God in whomsoever I served." The *guru* blessed him and said: "You have understood the essence of my religion: others only swear by it."

In the Sikh war of independence after the death of their
last *guru*, the Sikh leadership saw to it that no one was perse-
cuted on account of his caste or creed. Guru Nanak when
asked what his caste was replied:

> There are the lowest of the low-born, and with the least
> of these, Nanak identifies himself, for what has he to do with
> the high and mighty? Wheresoever the poor and the lowly
> are cared for, there also raineth the mercy of God.

The entire Sikh movement saw to it that it is the least of
the community who are thrown up as social leaders, military
commanders, men of affairs, and spiritual guides. Having
tasted discrimination and tyranny based on caste and religion,
the Sikh movement overcame the temptation to fall into it.
Under Ranjit Singh, the Sikh emperor who built a large
empire to the northwest of India, Muslims were the equal
partners in the highest councils of the state along with the
Hindus. Large endowments were made for the building of
the new mosques, or the maintenance of the old. The death
penalty was abolished, perhaps for the first time in history.
Very generous pensions and land grants were offered to those
who were dispossessed as a result of the Sikh conquest. When
in 1849 came the fall of the Sikh kingdom at the hands of the
British, the Hindus and Muslims fought shoulder to shoulder
with their Sikh brethren for their honor and in defense of
freedom. Today the Sikhs are found in almost every part of
the world and are honored for their catholicity of outlook,
for seeing good in, and cooperating with every nation with
whom their lot is cast. In their own country, they have fought
for independence under the great leadership of Mahatma
Gandhi and suffered disproportionately to their numbers; they
imbibed his teachings (for they are so close to the teachings
of the Sikh religion) of the indivisibility of man and the indivisibility of peace. As against the time-honored aphorism
that "nothing succeeds like success," the *gurus* enjoined that

"nothing fails like an undeserved success." A glorious defeat is far better than an immoral victory.

"In his defeat, the God-conscious winneth against the whole world. He alone loses who loses his goodness of heart," proclaimed Nanak.

Gandhiji's doctrine of nonviolence, even in the face of greatest provocation, was indeed in the blood of every Sikh, his *gurus* having suffered martyrdom without a word of regret or approbation even against their persecutors. When, in the campaign of Guru-ka-Bagh in the early nineteen twenties, the Sikhs suffered brutal assaults from the police and did not raise a finger in return, that great Christian leader, C. F. Andrews, remarked: "I see a Christ being crucified in every Sikh before me."

Gandhiji's work for Hindu-Muslim unity and for the abolition of untouchability and the distinctions of the rich and poor by making the rich trustees of the poor, touched the heart of every Sikh, as these teachings were part of the Sikh heritage. "He who eats, must work; he who lives must be self-dependent," have also been a part of the Sikh credo through the centuries. The Sikh *gurus* were all householders, they worked with their own hands for their livelihood and then shared what they had with others, as every Sikh is expected to do. They kept themselves in readiness to sacrifice even their lives and those of their dear ones in defense of man's inner autonomy. Perhaps Sikhism can claim the most credit for having fought for the rights and privileges of others at the expense of their own. Guru Nanak, the founder of the faith himself, suffered imprisonment at the hands of Babur, the founder of the Mogul empire. Strangely enough, the *guru* bewails the lot of both Hindus and Muslims through his powerful verse compositions of protest against this onslaught. What is more, though the *guru* saw the devastation only of the Punjab at his hands, he never in his entire writing mentions the word Punjab. It is always the agony of the entire "Hindustan" that claims his compassion. Guru Gobind Singh in his compositions blesses every country and community by name for being the devotees, each in its different way, of the one and the only God.

Is it a mere coincidence of history that the year 1969 in which we celebrate the centenary of Gandhiji we shall also be celebrating the quincentenary of Guru Nanak, the founder of the Sikh faith? God works his miracles in mysterious ways.

Sikhism believes in one God and one man irrespective of his caste, creed, sex, color, country of origin, dress, diet, peculiar habits, or ritual. It affirms that no sure peace is possible or desirable if it denies even to a single man his liberty of conscience, or if one group dominates another, either politically, socially, economically, or through religious imperialism. Man has to sacrifice his ego and his interests in the service of his family; the interests of his family in the interest of his nation; the interests of his nation, in the service of mankind. Not merely should he do unto another what he wants done by him, but irrespective of reward, he must perform his *dharma*, which is that all life is pure and sacred and has the same divine spark illuminating it from within.

We talk too much nowadays in terms of separating religion from politics, but unless *dharma* (not theology or dogma) becomes the mainstay of the polity of nations, individually and collectively, man is sure to destroy his race, or—what is even worse—to keep him in perpetual fear of his neighbor. Coexistence is therefore the only alternative to nonexistence. The other man's point of view is as sacred as my own. But unless I am prepared to suffer and sacrifice for these noble ideals, as the Sikh *gurus* did, there seems little hope for peace in the world. For this, men of faith, no matter to what denomination they belong, will have to get together on a single platform and ridding themselves of the academics of their personal theologies make religion also a fit instrument for the secular uplifting of man. Whatever the merit of our individual philosophies, unless they can be of some concrete use to the world of the living, religion will cease to be of any interest to the average man.

Ramana Mahirishi recalled that a certain philosopher was being rowed across a river. As is the habit of such philosophers, he asked the boatman if he knew the science of the stars. The boatman replied in the negative. The philosopher said, "Then you have wasted one-fourth of your life." He asked again, "Do you know logic—inductive or deductive?" The boatman replied, "No. I know nothing of it." The philosopher said, "You have wasted half of your life in vain." Then he questioned him again, "Do you know any history, geography, or the science of polity?" And the boatman said, "No, I know nothing about these either." "Then you have wasted three-fourths of your life," repeated the philosopher angrily.

Soon thereafter the river rose and there was a great tempest and the boat tossed about helplessly on the angry waters. Now it was the turn of the boatman to ask: "Sir, do you know how to swim across the tumultuous waters?" The philosopher, dejected and humbled, said, "No." Thereupon the boatman laughed and said, "Then you have wasted the whole of your life, for while I shall swim across, you will be drowned!"

Men of religion should seriously ponder this story.

5. ✍ SANCTIONS FOR PEACE (II)

THE FOURTH SESSION of the Symposium was also devoted to explorations of sanctions in still other religions for peace. Rabbi André Zaoui of the Liberal Israel Union of Paris was chairman. Four papers were presented, after which there was again discussion.

VIRA SHAIVISM: HINDUISM

Jagadguru Shri Gangadhar Rajayogeendra Mahaswamiji Moorusavirmath, Hubli

INDIA IS REPUTED to be the land of saints and sages. Foreigners so regard it and not without reason. Centuries before the Christian era, before any other religion had come to birth, our forefathers had composed the Vedas, the Āgamas, and the Upanishads. They shaped the Varna-Ashrama Dharma and codified the Manu Dharma Shastra (which is the basis of social organization), discovered the *summum bonum* of life—here and hereafter—and developed a civilization and a way of life securing human welfare. It will be no exaggeration to say that India has been the source of religion for the rest of the world. Some of the world's great religions, like Islam and Christianity which originated elsewhere, have thrived under the Indian sky. India has come to be regarded as the nursery of philosophies (*darshanas*) of many schools. To the Indians, the spiritual is paramount; the material secondary. Since the time of the civilization of Mohenjo-Daro and Harappa, some 3,000 years before the Christian era, various philosophies have been springing up on the Indian soil. The schools of Chārvāka, Jainism, Buddhism, Sāṁkhyā, Yoga, Pūrva Mīmāṁsā, and Uttara Mīmāṁsā have all arisen and flourished in India. The six systems of Indian philosophy are famous the world over. Besides those six systems, another—the Mrida Darshana—has come down to us from a remote antiquity. That is the Shaiva Dharma. Shiva is the presiding deity of the Shaiva Dharma. Though *shiva* and *rudra* were terms of different significance at the beginning, in course of time they have become synonyms. If *shiva* stands for or symbolizes good, *rudra* stands for or symbolizes the terrible. This distinction occurs in certain contexts of the Rig Veda. Some antiquarians hold that the Mohenjo-Daro civilization, which is anterior to the Rig Veda, leans to Shaivism.

From the point of view of antiquity, Shaivism is at least as old as the Veda and the Upanishads, and it was equally widespread. *Shivaliṅgas*, worshipped by the Shaivites, are to be found not only in India but in many other lands. It has been conjectured that the worship of the *liṅga* or the *phallus* was in vogue in Cambodia, Champa, Indonesia, China, Japan, and other eastern lands before 515 B.C. It is known that near the mountain regions in Central Asia the worship of the *liṅga* prevailed. Thus Shaivism is at once the oldest and the most widespread of religions.

The twenty-eight Shaivagamas comprehending the Kamika and the Vatula are the authentic canon of the Shaiva Dharma. In the Sūkshma, the Vira, and other *agamus*, there is mention of the seven denominations of the Anadi Shaiva, Ādi Shaiva,

Mahā Shaiva, Aṇu Shaiva, Antara Shaiva, Pravara Shaiva, and Antya Shaiva. But these seven identical denominations are not mentioned in all the *agamas*. While the first four, namely, Anadi Shaiva, Ādi Shaiva, Mahā Shaiva, and Aṇu Shaiva, are mentioned as such, the remaining are substituted by Yoga Shaiva, Jñāna Shaiva, and Vira Shaiva. Shri Tontada Siddhalinga Shivayogi (1475 A.D.) who has authoritatively expounded the Vira Shaiva doctrine, after enumerating the six sects of Ādi Shaiva, Mahā Shaiva, Aṇu Shaiva, Antara Shaiva, Antya Shaiva, and Pravara Shaiva, omits reference to the Anadi Shaiva and substitutes the Vira Shaiva in its place. It can therefore be inferred that the Anadi Shaiva, mentioned in the Shivagamas, is a synonym for Vira Shaiva. It becomes evident that six schools of Shaivism have adopted varna ashrama, while Vira Shaivism transcends varna ashrama.

Among these Shaiva variations, three are major: Kāshmīr Shaiva, Tamil Shaiva, and Vira Shaiva. It is customary to designate the Kāshmīr Shaiva as the Trika or the Pashupatha mata, the Tamil Shaiva as the Shaiva Siddhānta, and the Vira Shaiva as the Shat Sthala. If the Trika and the Shaiva Siddhānta uphold Shiva Sāmānata Vāda or the doctrine of coequal status with Shiva, Vira Shaivism upholds Shaiva Samarasya. Though the Jivatma, being purged of the triple impurity (*mala traya*), attains a pure state, becomes immersed in the effulgence of Shiva and seems lost to view, his independent existence as an entity abides. From one standpoint this would seem to support *dwaita* or dualism.

Vira Shaivism inculcates liṅganga samarasya or complete oneness of *liṅga* and *aṅga*. Consecrated by the triple ministration of *veda*, *mantra*, and *kriyā diksha* and rid of the triple impurity of anava, karmika, and māyā, the bound soul realizes the true aspect of *liṅga* (*liṅga swarupa*). Aṅga means the pure-souled individual. By developing the *bhakti* or devotion within him by righteous action or *sat kriya*, by mingling or harmonizing it with the *shakti* or energy in *liṅga*, *aṅga* finally achieves *linganga-samarasya* or complete oneness of *linga* and *anga*. This is the liberation or salvation envisaged by Vira Shaivism. If Kāshmīr Shaivism and Tamil Shaivism favor *dwaitism*, Vira Shaivism favors *shivadwaita*. This is the difference, metaphysically speaking, the thirty-six *tatvas*, the *mala-traya*, and the *shadadhwa* being common to the three schools of Shaivism. But in other respects there are very many differences.

The worship of Shiva *shakti* is of great antiquity. The *shivalingas*, installed in the Shaiva temples throughout India, are a concrete form of the formless or *nirakara* Shiva and indicate that he is *svayambhu* or self-existent. It is the hallmark of the Shaiva Dharma to install this *shivalinga* or *sthavarlinga* in temples and shrines and worship it. But the worship of *ishtalinga* is an especial mark of Vira Shaivism. Conceiving the body to be the temple of God and seeking to make it a fit tabernacle, the Vira Shaiva wears on his body the *ishtalinga* as the symbol of the eternal *parashiva* and never parts with it. This is the symbolism of the *ishtalinga: parashiva* who is not manifest to the eye does not abide in Kailas. He resides in the actual body. The body must be consecrated as a temple; it must be experienced as *maha kaya*. Indeed, it should prepare for the creation of *vishwa kaya*. In it the entire essence of spiritual life must be embodied. The core of our being must profoundly experience and get merged in *parashiva*. That the mystic life should be a sort of stage and sporting ground for universal life and universal place which are animated by the vision divine of the Lord—this is the mystery of the ritual of the *ishtalinga* worn on his body by the Vira Shaiva. *Shat-sthala* is the soul, *panchachara* the life, and *ashtavarna* the body for Vira Shaivism. In the order of *bhakta, mahesa, prasadi, pranalingi, sharana,* and *aikya,* the *sādhaka's bhakti, shraddha, nishta,* etc., assume the forms and progressively become merged in *shakti*. At first, that is, from the *bhakta-sthala,* all *kriyā* performed with *shraddha,* that is, with devotion and dedication, becomes *liṅga*, *chitta* becomes *suchitta*. It is this *suchitta* that transforms *padārtha* into *prasada*. In Vira Shaivism this process of integration, whereby *padartha kaya* becomes transformed into *prasada kaya*, is cardinal. Much importance is attached to the psychological conversion or change. Vira Shaivism is a psychological approach to God. *Aṅga* who is a portion of the divine receives from the sacred person of the *guru* a *liṅga* which is token of the knowledge of his (*aṅga*) real self, and worships it. Then begins the *bhaktasthala*. From the moment the aspiration to possess the *ishtaliṅga* is born, the *jīva* or the soul cast into the vortex of the world after a round of births and deaths begins to long for emancipation. Then he feels the consciousness of the God hidden in him.

The love that blossoms in a virgin of sixteen does not enter from outside; it has been there latent in the virgin's consciousness from birth. As time passes, it sprouts, buds, blossoms, and bears fruit. The energy that manifests itself as an ear of corn lies there hidden in the sap of the plant. In the embryo of the peacock are concealed all the hues that burst into glory afterwards, and all its parts and limbs. Even so is the infinite energy of the divine (Paramātma) embedded in the *jīvātma*. It is the goal of the Vira Shaiva to manifest this latent power and attain the original splendor. Here integration is regarded as more important than liberation. In the process of evolution when the individual becomes aware of the power of the Lord hidden in him, he feels a sort of disgust or repulsion for the external world of the senses which holds him in its grip. In truth both the *ātma tatva*, which is the reality of the *jīvātma*, and the *prapancha tatva*, or the world of senses which environs the *jīvātma*, have issued out of the identical *mahaliṅga*. *Ātma* gets involved in the world with which it has no relation and, as *jīvātma*, becomes subject to the flux in the world and gets caught in the revolving wheel. When it becomes conscious of its original truth or reality, then is born the desire to free itself from the bondage of the world which now inspires a feeling of repulsion or disgust. He begins to realize that his is a dog's life helping itself to chance crumbs. Life becomes a bed of torture; he lives in the shadow of death. Tossed about and battered by the circumstances of life, the *jīvātma* seeks refuge in the Lord. He turns in supplication to the divine.

To the devotee who thus surrenders himself with a single undivided mind, *guru karunya* is vouchsafed. The *guru* who represents the divine hastens down to the disciple in response to his call. The pure-souled *guru* places his benedictory hand on the head of the disciple, contemplates him with his eye of knowledge, rouses the power latent in the disciple, converts it into *bhava* and crystallizes it into *bhavaliṅgi*, converts it into life, crystallizes it into *pranaliṅgi*, and then vouchsafes to him the gross form of *ishtaliṅga*. Now the disciple becomes eligible for *veda*, *mantra*, and *kriya* initiations. As the outcome of the initiations he acquires the *ishtaliṅga*. The *ishtaliṅga* is the symbol of the *shakti* of the divine pervading the entire animate and inanimate universe, the world and the sky and the abyss below; and at the same time this *shakti* is immanent in him. This is the knowledge of the real self. Now the *ishtaliṅga* which comes into his *karasthala* as the object of his worship is none other than his own real self. To the neophyte an object of worship is necessary in the initial stages. The object of worship at this stage seems to be external. It is the object of meditation, concentration, and adoration of the *bhakta*, but, in truth, the worshiped and the worshiper, the adored and the adorer, the *bhakta* and the *deva* are one and the same. *Bhakti* is transformed into *shakti*; *bhakta* into *deva*, that is, reality is attained. Here *bhakti* is not an instrument for liberation. It is biune, the complete oneness of *liṅga* and *aṅga*, *liṅgaṅga samarasya*. This is beatitude, the supreme good. Its goal is the transmutation of *bhakti* into *shakti*, of *padārtha kaya* into *prasad kaya*. This is the *shatsthala* discipline or path. For this discipline, *prana* and *bhavaliṅgas* have been established in the *sthūla* (gross), the *sūksma* (subtile), and the *karana* (causal) bodies respectively; they are based on *āchāra shadliṅgas* and the *nasikadi shadindriyas* (nose and other organs and senses). *Aṅga* assumes three forms as *tyaganga*, *bhoganga*, and *yoganga*.

The devotee who has developed a distaste or disgust for the world or saṃsāra is however not in a position to reject or renounce it. Vira Shaivism affirms the reality of the world. It declares the superiority of the world as the *karmodyoga bhumi* or the scene of labor and activity to the *bhoga bhumi* and the *bhoga tanu* or the field of enjoyment and the body of enjoyment. It posits that to attain the *para* (other, beyond), the *iha* (here), is necessary. So the devotee bent on the path of salvation or *moksha* should not despise the world and flee it, but hold fast to it and seek salvation in and through it. The world must become the means for the attainment of *paramārtha* or the supreme good. Thus it cannot be abandoned, neither can it be clung to; one cannot abide therein, nor can withdraw from it. A key to this paradox has to be discovered. That key is to direct our affairs not with the motivation of the senses, but with *liṅga* orientation. Sense-indulgence begets the dualities of heat and cold, happiness and misery to which the *jīvātma* becomes subject.

The Gītā makes this lesson clear. In the *shadindriyas*, *shadliṅgas* have been located so that the activity of the senses can be changed into the activity of the *liṅga*. All the experience that comes through the senses—sound, touch, form, taste, and smell—has to be transmuted into *prasada*. In this process *chitta*, *buddhi*, *ahaṅkāra*, *manas*, *jñāna*, and *bhāva* by the alchemy of *bhakti* and *āchāra* are turned into *suchitta*, *subuddhi*, *nirahankara*, *sumanas*, *sujñana*, and *sabhava*. It is through the door of the *chitta*, *buddhi*, *ahaṅkāra*, and *manas* that we experience the world. By the force of *āchāra* these instruments lose their original quality, i.e., the quality of *prakṛiti*, and acquire the quality of *prasada*. They become fit vehicles of *aṅga* and its activity, that is, a fit receptacle of *prasada*. This evolution continues as *bhakti* grows. *Bhakti* is fostered by *sadachara; sadachara* itself springs from *sujñāna*. If the Vedānta declares "*jñāna devato kaivalyam,*" Vira Shaivism declares that unless this knowledge is turned into experience, no *kaivalya* or salvation is possible. That means that knowledge must be translated into action or *kriyā*. Knowledge which does not issue in action and action which is not inspired by knowledge are sources of bondage. So knowledge and action have to be harmoniously combined. From this harmony results the harmony of *bhakti* and *shakti*, the harmony or complete oneness of *linga* and *anga*. That is the content of the Vira Shaiva *shatsthala*. This is the experience yielded by the disciplines of *bhakta, mahesha, prasadi, pranalingi, sharana,* and *aikya*.

It can now be considered how Vira Shaivism by this practice makes world peace practicable. In the individual, as in the world at large, desire is the root cause of any unrest that shows itself. The individual who has rooted out desire enjoys bliss everywhere. It is an eternal truth that desire is the root cause of misery. As desire and ambition become the cause of clashes between individual and individual, so too they precipitate conflict among the nations. Desire, greed, and ambition turn into selfishness which seeks appeasement and gratification, no matter if, as a consequence, the nation is hurtled into violence and injustice. Self-aggrandizement leads to ruthless policies. It is this impulse that actuates the attempt of the big powers to swallow up the smaller nations. Owing to the uncurbed play of selfish and ambitious impulses, there develops a conflagration of war which is a peril to culture and civilization.

The many wars in the past, and the two world wars in our own generation are pointers in this direction. Vira Shaivism has explored a way of uprooting ambition and selfishness. A *sādhaka* of this persuasion must learn to do away with likes

and dislikes equally and remain in the world but not of it. If
he acts according to his likings, he will convict himself of
selfishness. Such selfishness becomes a titanism and wrecks
the world. The feeling of dislike leads to inertia and inaction.
The world can advance and reap all around prosperity only if
there is a dynamic urge. Selfishness has to be eliminated. Inaction must cease. That means that all transactions between
individual and individual, between nation and nation, must be
controlled by a higher ethic and be regarded as a discipline in
obedience to a higher *shakti*. Abandoning likings and dislik-
ings, the individual participates in the affairs of the world in
dedication to *linga*, for *lokasangraha*. If each individual and
each nation develop this consciousness of functioning for
linga, then it becomes *lokasangraha*. If all the nations of the
world abjure selfishness and egoistic ambition this way, and
activize themselves disinterestedly for *lokasangraha* and *viswa
sangraha*, peace automatically follows.

Inaction must cease. Vira Shaivism has discovered the
efficacious gospel of *kayaka*. It can be said that *kayaka* is the
great gift of Vira Shaivism to world peace. Vira Shaivism enjoins *kayaka* or work on everyone. One has to work all one's
life. From the Brahmin to the Pariah, one and all must toil.
Live on the sweat of your brow. Vira Shaivism condemns
one's living at the expense of another. In the Vira Shaiva
scheme, there is no room for idleness, inaction, inertia, mendi-
cancy, and social parasitism of any kind. It is a sin to eat the
bread of idleness; it is virtue to toil for one's bread. As each
individual is enjoined to support himself by his work, it becomes the duty of society to provide work for each individual. The individual toils for society; society takes upon itself
to insure the welfare of the individual. As it is the portion of
the individual to work for society, so it is the portion of
society to guarantee individual well-being. In this order, society can steadily advance from strength to strength without

being checkmated by unemployment and unrest resulting therefrom. Vira Shaivism which makes work imperative also provides an exalted conception of work. Whatever the work we engage in, it is dedicated to the divine. There is no high or low in respect of work, nothing noble or ignoble. Toil at the forge, labor at the mill, work at the loom; all have an equal value in the eyes of the Lord. In the conception of the Vira Shaiva, every winking of the eye is the functioning of *linga*. Where, then, is the difference of high and low? All activity of the body, *anga*, is activity of *linga*. As such, work is of the nature of the divine. "Work is worship"—that is the motto on the high-flying banner of Vira Shaivism. If every nation occupies itself with the work before it, where will arise the need or occasion for interference in the affairs of others? It is worthwhile further to examine the implications of this philosophy of work. Work, everyone must. Attitude to work is all in all. Work for the *linga*. Unto the day, the day's work. Lay not up for the morrow.

The fruit of today's toil conserved for tomorrow is stale, bitter, poisonous.

This desire to save, conserve, and accumulate is at the root of the unrest in the world. If this is extirpated, then peace settles and can be consolidated in the mind of the individual, the territorial extent of the country, and the world stage.

The lives of the Vira Shaiva *sharanas* abound with events and episodes testifying to the potent efficacy of the doctrine of *kayaka*. Sharana Marayya was ruler of Kashmir in the twelfth century. He forsook his kingdom and came to the high abode of Basavanna of Kalyan. There he took up the work of carrying loads of fuel and maintained himself out of what he earned as *prasad*. One day Basavanna in disguise visited Marayya's home in his absence, partook of *prasad*, and left behind a piece of gold. At the sight of this gold, Marayya flew into a passion exclaiming, "Whatever a *sharana* touches

turns into gold. This bit of gold I find here, not being the
product of true, disinterested toil, is not acceptable." So saying he flung it away.

Another *sharana* of the same name came to be known as
Ayada Akki Marayya, as he was given to collecting rice grain
found in the streets. Daily he used to collect as much rice grain
as was necessary for the day. One day when he brought home
his wallet full, his wife Lakkamma remarked that it was
sacrilege for *amareshlinga* to have collected in excess of the
day's needs and returned the superfluous quantity.

These episodes bring out the sentiment cherished by the
Vira Shaivas in regard to *satya shuddha kayaka*, the conception of work that has its roots in truth and disinterestedness.

Be he prince or potentate, bodily labor is obligatory. There
should be no hoarding or collecting the earnings of labor.

At work, one ought to forget even the *guru*, even the
linga, because work is worship, "*kayakave kailasa*." Work is
not here to be understood as a mere means; it is itself "*kailasa*"
divine. The joy that flows from true and disinterested work is
joy ineffable, *paramananda*. There is little doubt that peace
can be permanently established in the world through this
gospel of *kayaka* or work that has its roots in truth and disinterestedness.

While working or accepting the reward therefor, every
worker must practice the spirit of total surrender and dedication. Vira Shaivism lays it down that *tanu* (body), *mana*
(mind), *dhana* (wealth), must all be offered to *guru-linga-
jangama*—to the *guru* who is the image of Sat, *linga* which is
the image of Chit, and Jangama who is the image of *Ananda*.
It is *Sat-Chit-Ananda*, the supreme divine, who manifests himself for the good of the world as *guru-linga-jangama*. The
bhakta has to incorporate in his own *kaya* or vehicle the triad
of *guru-linga-jangama*. That is to say, he has to cleanse himself
of the limitations which are the outcome of the three impurities
of *anava*, *karmika*, and *maya*—namely, diminished dimension,

diminished energy, and diminished knowledge and grow into all-pervasiveness, all-might, and all-knowingness. To encompass this he has to become a *dasohi* of three types. The *guru-jangama* must distribute the benefit in society and labor for *lokasangraha* or the good of the world. In this social scheme, mutual good is the dominating motive: *ātma-kalyana*, the welfare of the individual; *loka-kalyana*, the welfare of the world —both these objectives are realized. Is not such a scheme conducive to world peace?

The genuine Vira Shaiva devotee has to develop into a *dasohi* of three types. Not *"so'ham"* but *"dasoham"* is his high motto. In other words, humility is the very basis of his personality. This humility is the foundation of society, too, according to Vira Shaivism.

"No one lesser than me, no one greater than a devotee of Shiva. Thou art the witness for this, O Kudala Sangama Deva."

If we consider these utterances of the *sharanas*, it becomes clear that service or *"kainkarya"* is the very breath of Vira Shaivism. The more the individual assimilates this spirit of service and devotedness, the more he grows in stature. This spirit saves nations. Ambitious and aggressive nations trampling smaller nations under foot will bite the dust one day. A policy of "live and let live"—the outcome of humility—will raise nations as well as individuals to glory. Such an attitude helps building up peace, order, and plenty in the world.

Equality is a fundamental rule of life with the Vira Shaivas. Historically Vira Shaivism represents a revolt against caste which shook the very fabric of Indian culture. It sought to uproot the inequality of caste. In its place Vira Shaivism recognized all as equal—the high caste and the low caste together. Vira Shaivism does not countenance the gradations and degradations of the caste system. The Shiva *bhaktas* form one universal community; devotion to Shiva is the bond of society. Casteism and racialism have been the bane of the world, as history evidences. The oppression of the Negro in the West and the untouchables in India are but two instances of insensate social discrimination. Scores of *vachanas*—the utterances of *sharanas*—can be cited in favor of equality between man and man, between man and woman, and among all, irrespective of caste, creed, sex, and status. Equality is the bedrock on which world peace must be founded.

Liberty is the birthright of every individual. Vira Shaivism heeds this fundamental truth. The *ishtalinga* to be found on the person of every Vira Shaiva is the imprimatur of the religious liberty everyone enjoys. It signifies social freedom too. It is the goal of the Vira Shaiva to safeguard this liberty whereby one is not reduced to dependence on another, and each pursues his way without servility in relation to others.

Fraternity is equally the essence of Viswa Dharma, the religion of humanity. All who wear *linga* on the *anga* constitute a confraternity and are equal in the eyes of Sangamanath (God). As a *vachana* illustrates, it is love of and devotion to Shiva that draws men together and proves to be the strongest link of brotherhood. Vira Shaivism wholly approves of the great injunction, "Love thy neighbor as thyself." It approves with good reason because all are sparks of the divine, Shivamsa-Sambhuta. World unity and world peace become assured in the wake of the recognition of the identity of the one self in all.

The Vira Shaivas have striven to apply equality and fraternity at all levels, in social relations and the pattern of individual life, and thereby they have heralded a social revolution. The Shiva *sharanas* of yesterday found an easy solution for the economic malaise which has baffled French and Russian social and political workers, and this they achieved 800 years ago, clearly formulating the concepts of liberty, equality, and fraternity. This social gospel should pave the way for world unity or peace.

Daya (kindness) holds a key to the solution of all discords.

If only a little humanity infuses itself in individuals and nations practicing persecution and cruelty, the atmosphere will clear of its own accord. It is only when humanity or kindness is eclipsed and driven under that dark forces prevail. Vira Shaivism is the religion of humanity. Bassava held *daya* or humanity to be the taproot of all *dharma; dharma* bereft of *daya* is no *dharma*. Practice *daya* or kindness to all living creatures, said Bassava. The opposite of *daya* is *himsa* or violence and cruelty. Basavanna's message of *daya*—positive kindness and positive service—brings peace to the world by ruling out aggression and acquisitive fury.

Vira Shaivism sets much store by *achara*. There is no heaven apart, no earth apart; *achara* is heaven and *anachara* is hell; that is the substance of a saying and shows the status accorded to *achara*.

Ruled by *sadachara*, if one acts conformably to one's speech, the cycle of life will be completed here and now. Great stress is laid on conduct in accordance with profession; individuals as well as nations profess one way, and act another way. Hence the tragic consequences. In the political sphere the hiatus between speech and act is especially noticeable. Politics and religion should work in concert with each other. Religion must inspire political action; the sage, the unselfish man, the man of wisdom, should guide the statesman, the practical man, the man of action. Basavanna set an example in statecraft by accepting to act as the chief minister of the Kalachurya Samrajya where he strove to establish the kingdom of God on earth. The *sharanas* effected a transvaluation of values by seeking to work out their destiny here on earth, making it the home of peace and prosperity.

With the idea of giving universal currency to the tenets of Vira Shaivism, the great reformer and renovator of religion, Shri Basaveshwara instituted in the twelfth century the Anubhava Mantapa which may be likened to a lake of philosophy in which disported many a *paramahamsa*. In this way

Basavanna served to awaken humanity at large. At one stroke
were abolished the sects and schisms in society, the notion of
superior and inferior. Condemning the meaningless prolifera-
tion of custom, blind belief, and ritualism, and declaring the
primacy of universal good, Shri Basaveshwara provided a platform for spiritual discourse and discussion in the Anubhava
Mantapa in which *sharanas* and *sharanis* freely participated.
It will be no error to characterize the Anabhava Mantapa of
the day as the University of Shiva Jñāna, spiritual illumina-
tion. The central problems of life concerning humanity,
peace, and commonweal were threshed out in the light of their
religious experience by these earnest and purposeful men and
women gathered by the thousand in the historic assembly
of the Anubhava Mantapa. Especially they pondered and
discussed in this hall the themes of "Work Is Worship"
("*Kayakave Kailasa*"), "Humanity Is the Essence of Religion"
("*Dayave Dharmada Moola*"), and "Desire Is the Good of
All Humanity" ("*Sakala Jivatmarige Lesane Bayasu*"). These
epitomize the doctrines of service, humanity, and fraternity.
It is difficult to find a parallel to this achievement in the history of India or the history of the world. Some point as counterparts to this institution and activity the dialogues in Plato's
Academy, the output of Sangha Sahitya in the Tamil Nad, in
Upanishadic times, Janaka's Assembly, and, in historic times,
Ashoka's conventions or conferences. The conclusions of the
debates and deliberations conducted in the Anubhava Mantapa
have been systematized and condensed in "Sunya Sampadane"
which may be regarded as the handbook or manual of the
Anubhava Mantapa. What a wonderful vision the mantapa
presents! Here were collected men and women, young and
old, rich and poor, ignorant and learned, ignoring caste, color,
and language. They were united only by faith in the *linga*
and freely inter-dining, intermarrying, and sharing in the
spiritual banquet spread out to them in the pontifical presence
of Shri Allama Prabhu who presided over the assembly and

delivered the concluding word on the discussion. Here is light for the world of our own time wallowing in darkness.

In the main, Vira Shaivism did not arrive to exalt individuals or to chart a way of liberation for the individual.

Nor did it seek to startle or dazzle the populace by a *tour de force* exposition of any erudite philosophical dogma. The consolations of philosophy, the joy, the purity, and peace which flow from spiritual discipline or *sadhana*—the benefits of these should be opened to all. Instead of achieving world fellowship, to discard life here and fix one's thoughts on the beyond is the height of futility. The temporal and the spiritual, the here and the hereafter, are not mutually exclusive, but complementary and should be fused in a single, swelling harmony. These and such other are the basic beliefs of Vira Shaivism.

To bring the account to our own time it will not be inappropriate to refer to the personality and achievement of the late Shri Kumara Sivayogi who incessantly labored in the first half of this century to propagate the truths of Vira Shaivism on the basis of world peace. He founded, in pursuance of this object, the Shiva Yoga Mandir and the Akhila Bharatiya Veer-shaiva Maha Sabha. For this meritorious service the swamiji has been designated as *dwitiya basava*.

In summation, the four points of the heroic message of Vira Shaivism are: Do you all prepare to realize God? Do you all experience the fadeless bliss thereof? Do you all tend Godwards casting off the shackles of the ego? The gates of bliss of Shiva-Sukha are open to all—men, women, noble, and ignoble.

The fear of war envelops the world today. In the face of this menacing situation, the spiritual heads of all nations, philosophers, and statesmen should come together and deliberate on the best way to secure peace. The International Inter-Religious Symposium on Peace at this time is highly significant. As a result of such deliberations, world tension may be eased, the war clouds may roll away, and the sun of peace shine in the heavens, bringing hope to humanity. May all those who are spiritually inclined resolve that they will exert themselves in the cause of world peace and usher in the millennium. In this direction we shall all join in drawing into each one of ourselves the light of the many faiths of the world, centralize our energies for world peace, and immediately set about initiating the necessary steps.

CHRISTIANITY

Rt. Rev. John H. Burt

ANY ATTEMPT to delineate the sanctions in Christianity for peace ought to be undertaken only in the light of at least three historical factors.

First, the ethical teachings of Jesus of Nazareth grew out of the Jewish heritage into which he was born and in which he was raised. His concern for peace includes, therefore, the ancient Hebrew prophetic emphasis on human dignity and social justice. This is, of course, a common rootage shared with the Muslim.

Second, Christian moral theology through the ages has offered not a single but a variety of interpretations concerning how the peace ethic of Jesus should be applied to the problem of war. Although all the interpretations seek to be faithful to Christ's gospel of peace, contrasts between them have often resulted in the tragedy of Christians being pitted against Christians in a particular war.

Finally, Christians and sometimes their churches over the years have all too often failed to practice what their moral theology professes. Unholy wars have often been called holy. Even the name of Christ's cross has been used for unchristian conquest as in the Crusades.

This raises the problem of whether an essay on "Christian Sanctions for Peace" should deal simply with Jesus' pure teaching, with the churches' differing and often conflicting ethical applications, or with the actual record of Christians— a record that is full of unhappy and unfaithful chapters when it comes to war.

One thing is certain. There is a strong imperative for peace, or to be more precise, for the making of peace, at the heart of the Christian faith. This the founder of Christianity made abundantly clear. "Blessed are the peacemakers," said Jesus of Nazareth in the opening lines of his most celebrated sermon. Blessedness not simply for the peace lovers, or those with peace in their hearts, but "blessed are those" who in this strife-torn world make the peace, settle the strife, achieve the reconciliation. "Be ye doers of the word and not hearers only."

Reaching into his Judaic background, Jesus moreover affirmed that "love for one's neighbor" is a command second in importance only to the greatest requirement of all—love for God. The four gospel accounts (Mark, Matthew, Luke, and John) are brimming with variations on this peace theme. "Love your enemies. . . . Do good to them that hate you. . . . Pray for them which despitefully use you and persecute you. . . . Ye have heard that it hath been said, An eye for an eye and a tooth for a tooth, but I say unto you that ye resist not evil but whosoever shall smite thee on thy right cheek, turn to him the other also."

Now when the followers of Jesus, after his earthly ministry had ended, reflected on the way he himself lived in the light of those teachings they called him "the prince of peace." They remembered that "when he was reviled, he reviled not again." Particularly were they impressed that, in those days which proved to be his final ones, he resisted time and again attractive temptations to use his power and his personal popularity to overthrow oppression by the violence of revolution. To Peter, the disciple who drew the sword in defense of his master, Jesus rebuked him saying: "Put it away." Finally, from the very tree on which he was nailed for execution, Jesus showed no bitterness even toward those who put him there and said: "Father, forgive them for they know not what they do."

To be sure, there were other ethical imperatives which Jesus embraced with a fervor equal to that of peace. Social justice is one. He made it clear that peace is no substitute for seeing to it that the hungry are fed, the naked are clothed, and shelter is given to the homeless. Those acts of service set the standard by which our lives are to be divinely judged. Freedom for human dignity is another imperative elevated to preeminence. So it would be a mistake, therefore, to say that peace or peacemaking is the single central thing which Christian faith demands. A society ruled by the iron hand of tyrants is often peaceful even though it be despotic!

The peace which Jesus preached was not simply an inner peace, or a form of retreat from intense identification with the conflicts of the world. It was a peace based on justice. Moreover, his ethics for both peace and justice had a universal dimension—they are for everyone. It is significant that his final command to his disciples was not "go into Palestine or the suburbs of Jerusalem." It was "go into all the world and preach the gospel"—the gospel of peace.

This preaching, Jesus made clear, is costly. One must sacrifice for peace. Jesus said: "If anyone would be my disciple let him take up his cross and follow me. . . . He that taketh not the cross is not worthy of me. . . . He who would save his life for my sake must lose it. . . . Behold I send you as sheep into the midst of wolves, be ye therefore wise as serpents and harmless as doves."

Now history bears witness to the fact that the followers of Jesus, for the first three centuries, gave a quite literal and pacifist application to this teaching on peace. Not only did Christians refuse to enter active military service, but any who expressed even an intention of doing so were excluded from the ranks of the church. The two canons of Hippolytus in the middle of the third century are clear evidence that resistance to war was a stern discipline in the early church. Clement of Alexandria sums it up when he speaks of every Christian's call to a "royal priesthood" comprised of those "called to an army which spills no blood."

After the Edict of Milan in 313 A.D., the Emperor Constantine persuaded the church that preservation of the social order often requires force, and Christians began to see military service as not out of keeping with loyalty to the gospel if its intended purpose was to keep the peace. Yet for all this change, the church never forgot completely its pacifist origins; the constant demand for clerical exemption from war and the continuing creation of pacifist sects, through the centuries even until today, are illustrations that these origins were not forgotten.

Looking back over the 2,000 years of Christian history, it is possible to identify four general responses which Christians have made in trying to be faithful to Christ's command that we be peacemakers. These can be put into four brief phrases: the church over against the state, the church in unity with the state, the church separate from but parallel to the state, and the church in judgment on the state.

Interestingly, each of these four church-state relationships with regard to the problem of war has dominated at one or another period of Christian history. Each continues to find expression today in one or more of the Christian groups.

Those who embrace a position of absolute pacifism place "church over against the state." They display an unwillingness to participate in any acts of war whatsoever. This view characterized pre-Constantinian Christianity and is reflected in such contemporary churches as the Society of Friends (Quakers), the Mennonites, and the Church of the Brethren. For the pacifist, Christ's command to "love your enemies" and to "turn the other cheek" must be taken quite literally. Among many pure pacifists there is an implicit faith that somehow this witness, if embraced by sufficient numbers of Christians and other religionists, would be such a compelling demonstration to any warring nation as to make it stop fighting. Other pacifists, who hold no such pragmatic hope, believe, nevertheless, that faithfulness to Jesus' teaching on love and peace permit a Christian no other course.

A variation on this position is that of the vocational pacifist, who sees the peace ethic of Jesus as applying not universally to all men, but rather to those who choose to be his committed followers. Thus, while hesitating to recommend pacifism as a viable political strategy for his nation he insists that by embodying in his person a witness to peace he can do something to keep his war-involved nation from becoming blind to its own self-righteousness. Moreover, vocational pacifism has, over the centuries, had a high strategic value. Mahatma Gandhi himself drew some strength from it in developing nonviolent direct action in behalf of the India Freedom Movement. More recently in the United States, the civil rights movement under Dr. Martin Luther King, Jr., has made nonviolent civil disobedience a mighty weapon for correcting racial injustice. Dr. King's philosophy comes straight from a New Testament ethic interpreted in pacifist terms.

Just as Constantine, responsible for establishing public order in a far-flung empire, discovered that the *pax Romana* required the use of military strength and often war itself and persuaded the fourth-century Christians that deterrence by armed force and the anguish of armed conflict were often necessary to preserve the peace; so the majority of Christians from that day to this have rejected pacifism, believing it to be irresponsible in its understanding of the role of power. Although the Christian believes that man is sometimes capable of selfless love, his awareness of man's self-centeredness (his sin) alerts him to his own tendency to overvalue his own needs and claims and those of his nation. Because of these idolatries and imperfections in himself as well as in others, he knows that the pursuit of the good life in general and of justice in particular requires sanctions more reliable than those which the individual conscience can bring to bear on the behavior of men and nations one towards another. Thus, all orderly societies must have a system of law, sanctioned by coercive power—the power of police and the power of armies as well as the power of social mores and morality.

One form of this nonpacifistic response to the peace ethic of Jesus in Christian history is in the category of "the church in unity with the state." This view seeks to infuse the peace ethic into the very lifeblood of the nation itself, often through a union between church and state. "The church is the state when the state is on its knees." This view has a long history beginning in the decaying days of imperial Rome and flowering with the inauguration of the Holy Roman Empire by Charlemagne in 800 A.D. The temporal power of the state was subservient to the spiritual power of the church. Vestigial remnants of this tradition still linger in the Vatican state and the Church of England. Protestant Christianity reflected it also in the Geneva of John Calvin and some of the early American colonies.

The danger in such a church-state wedding, however, is all too often that either the gospel gets corrupted by the selfish concerns of the state or the church in her concern to run the state neglects her prophetic mission for social justice and peace. In many parts of the world, unfortunately, the result of this has led the state to silence the prophetic voice of the church with a requirement that Christ's gospel be strictly nonpolitical. This development is in the category of "the church separate from but parallel to the state."

This is largely the position of the Orthodox church today. The ecumenical patriarch in Istanbul may preside over the liturgical functions of the church, but he dare not publicly apply Jesus' teachings on peace and social justice to issues in the political order. He dare not rebuke the state after the tradition of Amos, Jeremiah, and Jesus. Other portions of Orthodoxy may relate the social gospel to the political order of the particular nation in which they exist. In either case the call for social justice is muted.

The fourth response of Christians to peace is "the church in judgment on the state." This is the prevailing view in most Protestant and most Roman Catholic churches today. It draws deeply on the tradition of the Hebrew prophets in calling the nations to account when they are callous in the treatment of the poor, when they betray freedom, when they too easily resort to war, or when they assume self-righteous postures. On the affirmative side this view also holds before the nations an appeal for those qualities making for human dignity which should be available to all men—liberty of speech and worship, equality of opportunity, the right to decent food, clothing, shelter, and basic health services. It is this sense of the church, or more precisely the gospel, standing above the nation, witnessing to a God for whom even the great nations of the world are as a drop in a bucket, that leads the Pope in Rome for example, to call on members of the United Nations to have "no more war," or to tell the President of the United States to stop the bombing of North Vietnam. It leads the National Council of the Churches of Christ in the U.S.A. or the World Council of Churches to say: "In the name of humanity, negotiate a peace in Southeast Asia and begin the work of reconstruction."

Let me suggest four strategies for peace in which Christianity might join with other world religions in striking at the underlying causes of war:

First, since Biblical faith holds that God is Lord of each nation and all nations and insists that all political institutions and policies are under his judgment, let Christianity join other religions in denouncing all national idolatry as the greatest obstacle to that reverence for all human life and respect for human dignity without which there can be no decent relations between nations. Let religion denounce the arrogance of any nation which engages in war save in self-defense or in aid of another nation which is the victim of aggression. Let religion insist on the universal right of the individual conscience not to engage in war.

Second, since the Christian moral imperative for peace is worthless unless it is translated into a social strategy that is relevant to the specific injustices in public life, let Christianity join with other religions in supporting the revolutionary ferment of the world today, offering specific, nonviolent ways to deliver God's people everywhere from poverty and hunger, racism, humiliation and oppression, and anarchy and war.

Third, since it is the Christian view that God is the creator of all things and that we are guests in his world and trustees of its natural resources, let Christianity join other religions in urging that we use our intelligence and knowledge in the making of a bountiful earth for all men, to develop and use the world's resources for human good, to protect and preserve the soil so that it will yield ample food, and to keep air and water free of poisons.

Fourth, since Christian teaching stresses the unity of all men under God, let it join other religions in asserting the primary allegiance of man to man, rather than man to government, in the family of man. Let world religion insist that human sovereignty precedes and transcends national sovereignty. Let us demand an end to anarchy in the dealings among nations. Let us demand that nations submit to laws among themselves, just as they require that their own citizens submit to laws within their own borders. We have the right to demand that the United Nations (or some other body) become the source of world law, replacing the irrational, irresponsible, and violent behavior of nations with orderly and workable methods for insuring a creative and just peace.

Is there any hope that any or all of these proposals can be achieved? Frankly, I see little practical possibility that they will be taken seriously enough or adopted quickly enough on the international level to work the revolutionary change in human attitudes we need overnight. The clock is ticking away the minutes as the nuclear race goes on. Christians are, however, a people of hope in the face of the darkest despair. Easter is the heart of their faith. And since there is no other way, why should we not try this road?

Twenty years ago a frail, poor, wizened man was shot in the back in this very city not very far from where we now deliberate. By the standards of the world he was a failure. He had neither health nor money. The cause of peace for which he worked was not achieved. Yet with all his frailties and weaknesses, he towers like a spirit over the lives of every person on this twentieth-century planet. The Prime Minister of India wept when he said: "In his death Gandhi has reminded us of the big things in life." What an epitaph! Who would not aspire to be such a magnificent failure rather than a tragic success in the kind of victory for which modern armies strive?

A psalm, common to the tradition of the Jew, the Muslim, and the Christian, reads: "Some trust in horses and chariots, but we will remember the name of the Lord our God." Many today say the only hope for peace is to be found in the modern version of "horses and chariots"—the bombs, the napalm, the jet fighters, and the rockets. So roll the drums; prepare for battle, the inevitable is on the march they say. But for the Christian and, I sense, for those at this table coming out of other religious traditions, the phrase is "we will remember." Yes, we will remember the name of the Lord our God. That is, we will reproduce the character of the Lord our God as we have seen him, for the Christian in Jesus, for others in some other revelation. For peace of mind and peace among the nations is ever and always "a fruit of the spirit" of God.

BUDDHISM

Ven. Baddeeama Wimalawansa Thero*

BUDDHISM IS A RIGHTEOUS PATH purely dedicated to the acquisition of world peace. The fundamental principle of Buddhism is to bring about peace and harmony in the world. The doctrine of emancipation as expounded in Buddhism can be categorized in terms of peace into two stages. The first stage is called relative peace and is technically known as *lokiya shanti*. This can be achieved in this complex world by organizing one's own mental disposition and keeping oneself fit to the external environment in accordance with the teaching of Buddha. The second stage is absolute peace or *parama shanti*. The achievement of this is parallel and simultaneous with the attainment of *Nibbaba*, the ultimate goal in Buddhism.

Peace in Buddhism in its relative sense is not an end by itself but a means to an end. In the absolute sense it is an end by itself.

The Buddhist answer to world peace is very clear but difficult to achieve. Yet without achieving it, no amount of treaties and pacts written on paper can produce real peace in the world. The first stanza of the Dhammapada teaches us that all unrest, all conflicts, and all disturbances are first born in the mind. War and conflicts are nothing but external manifestations of greed, hatred, ill will, violence, and ignorance born in the minds of men.

Conflicts born in the mind of an individual enlarge themselves into a social conflict and then into a national conflict and finally into an international conflict culminating in a great war. As there can be no society without individuals, there could be no social conflicts without individual conflicts.

---

* Composed with the help of Ven. Pimbure Soratha Thero.

Therefore the duty of peace-makers is to create a condition under which nations can live with less friction and individuals with less conflict. In order to create this condition, each individual should be provided with social, economic, moral, and spiritual security.

The Buddha has preached that it is an arduous task to be born as a human being and that no effort should be spared to make life happy and gay on a virtuous footing. A person deprived of the comforts of life will not have the peaceful environment which is essential for the achievement of absolute peace.

Poverty, disease, and ignorance have been referred to as three impediments to peace. In the Chakkavatti Sihanada Sutra, stealing, falsehood, and violence are referred to as three offenses resulting from poverty. It is also stated that in establishing peace in a country, the virtues, temperaments, schemes, and programs of the ruler could play a part of great importance. When the ruler becomes just and righteous, his ministers, soldiers, and subjects would also follow suit and in their turn ensure total peace. When the ruler becomes unjust, impatient, and unrighteous, the whole country becomes unrighteous and the extinction of peace will result.

Because there were oppressive rulers during the Buddha's time, as there are today, the Buddha preached tenfold virtues which should be adhered to by every good ruler:

1. The treasury of the state should be utilized for the welfare of the masses, according to necessity and without avarice. A ruler should not distribute the state income among his chosen friends, selfishly or with prejudice.

2. He should be of excellent character; he should act honestly and desist from falsehood.

3. He should sacrifice his surplus wealth and excessive comforts for the sake of the state.

4. He should not be prejudiced by craving, malice, fear, or delusion and should act in a straightforward manner.

5. He should be kindhearted toward the subjects.

6. He should lead a life of austerity.

7. He should not harbor malice.

8. He should not inflict pain on anyone and should never wreak vengeance.

9. He should be of moderate temperament, and should bear censure and praise alike.

10. He should respect public opinion.

When a ruler endowed with these tenfold virtues administers a country, it is certain that the people will enjoy peace and harmony. We come across several reigns of such kings in world history. Of these, the great Asoka era of India remains unsurpassed.

Another important factor for the establishment of peace is to rid the people of poverty. It is the duty of a state to fulfill the preliminary requirements of the people—food, clothing, and shelter. It is not possible for a person in hunger to observe virtuous principles. The Dhammapada gives a reference to an instance where the Buddha preached the *dhamma* to a hunger-stricken person only after providing him with a good meal to satiate his hunger.

The health of the public is another important factor in the maintenance of a society. Buddha said that health is the greatest treasure of man.

Education is yet another factor that is indispensable for the peace of a country. The Buddha has said that the uneducated man is like an uncollected person.

Similarly Buddha has preached of many other virtues conducive to the preservation of peace in a family, village, or institution. According to the Sigalovada Sutra, there should exist cordial relations between parents and children, teachers and pupils, husband and wife, relatives and neighbors, employer and employees, and clergy and laymen.

The breach of peace culminates in war between two countries. In analyzing the root cause of war, it may be observed that the cause is mainly the result of the wrongful path followed in consequence of defilements such as craving, ill will, and hatred. However, no one who participates in war takes the initiative to trace the fundamental cause and effect a remedy.

To one who investigates the basic causes of war and mutiny in the present world, there seems to be no recognizable difference between such causes and those in the Buddha's time. War is either the result of a desire for prestige or of territorial ambition. The cause for war also may be the result of a craving for conquering a country or a regional border dispute.

Reference is made in our scripture to an incident where the Buddha settled a war, having appeared himself in a battlefield. The paddy lands in the kingdoms of Sakyas and Koliyas in ancient India had been irrigated by the river Rohini. In the months of June and July of one year, a drought caused all the paddy fields in the Koliya kingdom to dry up, and it became essential that water should be obtained from the Rohini.

In pursuance of a treaty entered into previously, the right to water in that year was on the side of Sākyas. Because of this water dispute, the two kingdoms prepared for war. The armies headed by the two rulers took up positions on either side of the river. On learning of the situation, the Buddha, considering the calamity that would befall them in the event of war, arrived immediately at the spot and inquired as to the reasons which led them to war. When he was informed that the cause of the war was water, the Buddha preached about the futility of losing human lives so precious on account of some worthless water and thereby settled the dispute.

In another instance, when King Ajatasattu set out for war against the kings of Vajji, demanding his rights over certain village settlements given over as dowry to his mother, the Buddha advised the king and made him repair to his palace.

The Buddha has stated that nations are often dragged into

conflicts on account of slander and propaganda. Then it is the duty of intelligent men to ascertain the truth of such statements. The Buddha has referred to numerous such instances where propaganda has proved to be utter falsehood. He has shown that those men who declare war, breaking away from all bonds of peace and being deceived into believing false propaganda, have actually descended to the same level as animals. He has illustrated this preaching with examples from folklore. The story of the hare who slept at the foot of an apple tree is one such illustration. This story has been highlighted in sermons advising people not to be misled by frivolous incidents and false propaganda.

More often than not, mighty kings, being intoxicated with their power and wealth, wage war against small kingdoms governed by puny rulers. The story of the sparrow, who killed the elephant that reduced its nest to matchwood with the young chicks chirping therein, shows how the mighty ones come to grief by being intoxicated with power, that the weak should not be humiliated, and that consideration should be given to their strength also.

The worst threat to world peace is war, which according to Buddhist opinion is an adventure neither praiseworthy nor profitable. Buddha has preached that both parties at war would stand defeated at the end. "Victory breeds hatred." The winner would naturally incur the animosity of many persons while the loser would be buried in sorrow. Yet never would a person who engaged in war repent his conduct of violence after the conquest. The single instance of a personage who abandoned war forever after a remarkable victory was none but the Great Emperor Asoka. He was so remorseful for the dead in the battlefields that he ordered rock inscriptions to be set up bearing the words "no one shall wage war against another."

In order to establish permanent peace in the world, it is essential to adopt a procedure pertaining to the mitigation of defilements such as craving, hatred, and delusion. Every religious organization can be of immense service in achieving this ideal. Perpetual peace in this world could be obtained only by dispelling these defilements. The major part of Buddhist philosophy comprises discourses designed for the formation of a happy and peaceful nation.

The following requirements of the people should be fulfilled in order to stabilize peace in the world:

1. A program should be formulated to rid society of poverty.
2. Action should be taken to inaugurate schemes to produce ample supplies of foodstuffs for the people, schemes to be sponsored by both the state and the private sector.
3. While advice as to the prevention of diseases should be given, steps should also be taken to convince the people that cleanliness is an integral part of good living.
4. Facilities should be provided which would enable everyone to get a sound education.
5. People should be enlightened as to the ways of electing rulers capable of following the tenfold royal precepts.
6. A social reformation should be effected with a view to curbing defilements such as lust, hatred, and ignorance. All modes of propaganda should be used to achieve this end. Efforts should be made to build a society of men with very high ideals. For this purpose, school books, newspapers, and periodicals should be used.
7. Necessary steps should be taken to negotiate peace talks among the countries now at war.

JAINISM

Bool Chand

WHEN WE TALK OF RELIGION in relation to peace, we have to be clear in our mind about two things; peace at what level and peace for what purpose? Peace can be regarded from the point of view of the individual as well as from the point of view of the group. As far as the group is concerned, peace can be regarded from the point of view of the small religious fraternity or the national group, or of the large inter-communal, interracial, and international total world community.

Regarded from the point of view of the individual, I am not aware of any religion in the world which is more peaceful in its impact than is Jainism. It is a religion purely human in its origin; it emanated from the mouth of one who had secured omniscience and perfection by his personal effort, but who made no other claims for reverence. The condition he attained all human beings are entitled to attain, so long as they exercise self-control as he did and take action to shake off *karmic* matter from their soul. The foundation of Jain metaphysics consists in seven categories of fundamental ideas: *Jīva, ajīva, asrava, saṁvara, bandha, nirjara,* and *moksha.* The *jīva* or soul is a permanent and absolute substance, of which the chief characteristic is consciousness. In its pure state the *jīva* has unlimited perception, perfect knowledge, infinite power, and unbounded happiness. In our mundane world the *jīva* we find is surrounded by a large volume of fine matter called the *karma.* This *karma* matter can be attracted towards or weaned away from the *jīva,* depending upon the nature of the actions or deeds done. The Jain theory makes a detailed analysis of the types of deeds which would attract *karma* to the *jīva* and which would wean it away from it.

Ajīva is inanimate matter and *karma* is *ajīva,* but when it comes into contact with *jīva* it can bedim its power. It is a sort of infra-atomic particle of matter which produces changes in the *jīva* and these changes get into the organism to serve as the foundation of future action. *Asrava* deals with the *karma* that is acquired by *jīva,* in the manner in which the acquisition of further *karma* gets impeded. *Bandh* deals with the bondage of the soul by the *karma*, and *nirjara* is the process of the purging off of the *karma*. When *jīva* is freed from all *karma*, it gets released from the cycle of births and is said to attain *moksha*.

By the practice of the ethical way of life, of which minute details are given in Jain scriptures, we can secure the release of *jīva* from *karmic* matter. The Jain ethic is founded upon the principle of *ahimsā*. A Jain has not merely to refrain from violence, but he has to so order his life as to make the need to be violent superfluous. This principle of action has been well followed by the Jain community. Although the Jains are a small community in numbers (hardly three millions throughout the whole of India) and much scattered, they have continued to prosper where many other and larger communities have died out due to the hostility of other communities having still larger numbers. The peaceful tenor of life of Jains is almost proverbial, their benevolent activities directed to the good of all have earned them the goodwill of all the people.

The conception of an international community or a world order did not exist until rather recent times. Certain religions generally indulged in the sentimental dreams of an international community, and Jainism also has had its share of these. Since the idea of an international community did not exist, no religion could be expected to proclaim a world order, except perhaps in terms of the domination of that religion itself over the whole or a major part of the world. The concept of a Christian commonwealth arises from the consciousness that Christ won victory over the mundane world and over all that mars or hinders the spiritual well-being of men, but it is a commonwealth in which only Christian values will prevail.

Gilbert Murray said that in the late nineteenth century and early twentieth century the greatest supporter of peace in the world was the British government. That support was given in self-interest, for whatever might be the cause for the disturbance of peace, whether racial, economic, religious, or political, the germs for the spread of that disturbance to some area or other of the extensive British Empire might always be there. The policy of peace followed by those nations which are powerful or in control of large dominions is determined by their desire to maintain the status quo. Governments in those countries would no doubt seek the support of religion for their policy by giving it a moral appearance. But religion cannot come to the support of an existing order, unless that order is based upon the principle of justice. We have in our International Inter-Religious Symposium on Peace employed the term peace, knowing full well that where change appears unavoidably necessary for the securing of justice, peace would mean peaceful change and not just maintenance of the existing order.

Regarded from this standpoint, it would be well to search for an ideology which would truly favor the establishment of peace in the whole world. Representatives of all major religions of the world who met in Delhi in February 1965 for the Third General Conference of the World Fellowship of Religions found the essence of such an idea in *ahiṁsā*, which again is one of the basic tenets of Jain thought.

The following resolution on religion and *ahiṁsā* was unanimously passed by this general conference:

Love, truth, and non-attachment to worldly possessions are the essential constituents of Ahiṁsā. Ahiṁsā is the keynote of religion. Many religions of the world regard Ahiṁsā as the correct basic ideology of life, the others which do not go so far regard it as an effective methodology. The ideology of Ahiṁsā is based on sociality in human nature, and it is the basic social ethos comprehensive enough to afford guidance on all problems of human life. The methodology of Ahiṁsā is based on reverence for life. The World Fellowship of Religions believes that the proper and dispassionate study of

Ahimsā would give light to the world for the solution of our
difficulties, including those that pertain to inter-class, interracial, and international relations. This Third General Conference views with satisfaction the progress made in the
establishment of the Ahimsā Shodh-Peeth in Delhi under the
auspices of the Vishva Ahimsā Sangha and calls upon all
religious bodies and foundations throughout the world to
come to the assistance of Ahimsā Shodh-Peeth in making its
work the more fruitful and the more widespread.

The implications of *ahimsā* ideology are contained in the
resolution passed by that conference. *Ahimsā* ideology is
based on the ethos of sociality, and sociality naturally implies
reciprocity. All humanist thinkers all over the world, whatever may be their denominational profession, have preached
the ideology of *ahimsā* without actually using the term. In
India, of course, the term has been freely employed by the
Jains, Buddhists, and Hindus of practically all persuasions.
A clear distinction between *ahimsā* methodology and *ahimsā*
ideology was, however, made by the delegates to the general
conference. They specifically felt that *ahimsā* ideology was
really well fitted for the solution of intercommunal, interracial, and international conflicts and for the establishment of
a proper world order. It is by a proper and dispassionate study
of *ahimsā* that the world would get light, and for this purpose
an Ahimsā Shodh-Peeth has been set up in Delhi under the
sponsorship of the Jain Muni Sushil Kumar.

Our own Symposium might adopt the unique institution
set up through the efforts of the Jain Muni, and by doing so
they would be doing honor to the great name of Mahatma
Gandhi who so successfully employed the weapon of *ahimsā*
for the attainment of a specific political goal. The view that
ahimsā ideology has expressed in relation to war, as given in
a statement prepared by the director of Ahimsā Shodh-Peeth,
would be of special interest to participants of this Symposium.

There are those who argue that aggressiveness, being a

fundamental instinct of man, makes war an inevitable factor in human affairs. With such thinkers *ahiṁsā* philosophers do not agree.

Ahiṁsā believes first that aggressiveness is merely a derived instinct, and secondly, that even if aggressiveness of man were regarded as a primary instinct, it is quite easily possible to give to it an outlet that would provide personal satisfaction and yet not destroy society. A sociological analysis of war shows that war is in reality a stage in a cycle; the cycle of war, peace, and war again. In human societies this cycle takes more or less distinctive forms. In the beginning a strain or problem occurs in the normally peaceful and accommodative relations of sovereign states; this is followed by the development of what is called the war fever; after that hostilities begin, when military and international policies come to overshadow domestic ones and restrictions on free speech and freedom of assembly are willingly accepted; the newly developing situation is found to have effects on family, education, recreation, and other phases of community life; ultimately there is the termination of war with a general sense of relief and the urge to return to "normal" as quickly as possible. In this cycle the adjustment of individuals and groups to the conditions of war has to be made perforce. The psychological patterns of violent human behavior such as are noticeable in times of conflict are neither a natural nor a normal condition of men.

Living in a world in which violence between man and man is an unceasing fact of life, *ahiṁsā* philosophers have naturally concentrated their thought on the analysis of the causes of violence. At the same time the ethos of their integral thinking has been naturally directed to a society where violence would disappear and perfect harmony and integration would rule.

It is interesting to note that even the Marxists have been thinking along similar lines. They have sought to explain human conflicts in terms of economic interest and then concentrated their attention upon the ultimate establishment of a classless, nonviolent society—Socialism. The assumption of economic class interest as an explanation of all violence in human society appears wholly unrealistic to the *ahiṁsā* analysts. But a society based upon the idea of common good would be clearly nonviolent, from which war would be eliminated forever. That is the view of *ahiṁsā* philosophers as it is also of the Marxian socialists.

Slavery and war have been regarded as the two cancers of civilization by all thinkers from quite early times. The conquest of slavery in the early nineteenth century appeared to be a good omen for the prospect of a campaign against war. In this campaign against war neither the unrestricted economic individualism of the liberal school nor the totalitarian control of economic activities of the Marxist school was able to achieve any real success, although both had been preached as panaceas for over a hundred years. At one stage the modern western spirit of democracy gave mankind a new hope, but it was soon realized that even this hope cannot be fulfilled effectually until an international state is established.

As a result of the two world wars, the number of the great powers has been reduced from a fluctuating plurality to just two, namely the U.S.A. and U.S.S.R. Two is always an awkward number in any international balance of powers. The Russian and the American people are not very well equipped for understanding each other. In a world technologically unified, the competition for power beween the U.S.A. and the U.S.S.R. is going to be decided in the long run by those who are today reckoned as the developing nations. So long as the competition for power continues, it is quite clear that there can be no real elimination of war in the international sphere, however desirable it may be on humanitarian grounds.

The great German philosopher, Immanuel Kant, in an essay on "Perpetual Peace" written in the year 1795, stated several prerequisites for international peace: every nation should have a republican constitution, each people should possess national self-determination, there should be general disarmament, and there should be a federation of states agreeing to abolish war forever. Kant's program is as realistic today as when he formulated it, and it appears to be as far today from the realm of attainment as it was in 1795. Kant felt that the federation of states would have to take the form of a world republic.

Ahiṁsā thinkers feel quite emphatically that, beyond all questions of national self-interest, every people has a moral obligation to humanity as a whole. The *ahiṁsā* program is and has to be international in character and aim. It is only when a majority of the world's population come to see the underlying principles of *ahiṁsā* ideology that war as an institution and also as a weapon for the settlement of international disputes can be permanently abolished.

While aiming at the permanent abolition of war, however, *ahiṁsā* does not preach unthinking pacifism. It realizes that world peace involves the private renunciation of war on the part of an immense majority, and it does not therefore preach that men and nations should agree to submit to being the booty of others who do not renounce war. Nor does *ahiṁsā* countenance the cowardice of running away from dangers, should dangers come one's way in the pursuit of the path of peace and virtue. War itself may well be such a danger; and when involvement in a war takes place, *ahiṁsā* thinkers recommend that all rational steps should be taken with a view to sustain the morale of the army and the civilian population at the highest level.

Ahiṁsā thinkers have not failed to see that modern wars involve the complete mobilization of manpower and of the economic and industrial resources of the community. The distinction which formerly used to be made between the home front and the battle front has almost completely disappeared today. This is true with particular force in the countries in which the fighting actually takes place. In any future war, if the present lethal weapons are used, the industrial and production centers may become even more important targets than the *locus* of military forces. The need for sustaining civilian morale in wartime, therefore, becomes particularly great.

Psychologists have analysed that among the elements which help to sustain morale at a high level in a democracy are four: sound physical and mental health, marked by zest, ability to strive, a sense of humor, and a purpose in life; sound religious and spiritual values, involving the presence of a goal or aim to fight for the confidence and faith in ourselves; realistic understanding of our past and present situation, the gains to be obtained from victory, and the evil consequences of defeat; and lastly a sense of solidarity, including cooperation with all classes and groups in the community. *Ahiṁsā* thinkers support the cultivation of the above attitudes and strongly warn against apathy, distrust, scepticism, and the acceptance of the enemy values.

Ahiṁsā thinkers further recommend that all help should be given to ensure that the effects of a total war on family, children, and youth are the least harmful, and also that when war ends the return of the armed forces and of civilization to peace is untroubled. In our own country, *ahiṁsā* leaders have strongly recommended the formation of *shanti senas* for the above purposes.

Recognizing, however, that the waging of wars may be unavoidable for defensive, if not for offensive, purposes, *ahiṁsā* philosophers recommend that even more important than the elimination of war is the need to fight it by means which are free from violence. When Mahatma Gandhi had to wage a war against the British, with the object of freeing the country from their domination, he employed for this purpose only nonviolent weapons, including fasting, noncooperation, and the boycott of things British. The waging of war by such means necessarily involved great suffering for the whole people. This suffering was borne by all willingly and patiently, with the result that the waging of the war left no scars which remained unhealed. Despite the waging of a relentless war between the Indians and the British, the relations between the Indians and the British people are today cordial and happy. *Ahiṁsā* philosophers ascribe this happy result wholly to the fact that the weapons used on the side of the Indians were nonviolent (*satyagraha*).

How far it is possible to employ the weapons of *satyagraha* for waging a war against a foreign power in our present transitional stage is a question upon which *ahiṁsā* thinkers are not quite agreed. There are those who feel that *satyagraha* weapons can be as effectual and powerful against foreign aggressors as against domestic ones. In a statement made on August 29, 1939, Mahatma Gandhi said that he would advise Hitler to use *satyagraha* weapons in order to gain his just demands from the foreign powers of Europe. There are others who think that the use of *satyagraha* weapons alone in an international war would be unwise. Our own Indian government although generally committed to pursuing the policies of Mahatma Gandhi, the father of the nation, is finding it difficult to do away with the armed forces and to forsake recourse to arms. Among the Jain and Buddhist rulers in history also, the same difference of view is noticeable in the practice followed by Asoka and Kanishka among the Buddhist rulers, and in the practice followed by Sanprati and the rulers of Rajasthan in medieval times among the Jains.

6. ✍ THE RELEVANCE OF GANDHI AS A RELIGIOUS FORCE FOR PEACE

MEETING IN THE HOMELAND of Mahatma Gandhi, and co-sponsored by the International Seminars Subcommittee of the National Committee for the Gandhi Centenary, the Symposium naturally discussed the life and teaching of Gandhi. The sixth session of the Symposium, chaired by Bishop James K. Mathews, was opened with an Islamic service led by Peer Zamin Nizami Syed Bokhari. Shri G. Ramachandran, M.P., delivered a paper on "The Relevance of Gandhi as a Religious Force for World Peace." There were commentaries by three former associates of Gandhi: Kakasaheb Kalelkar, Pyarelal Nayar, and Prof. Nirmal K. Bose. In the midst of this discussion, Sheikh Abdullah of Kashmir, then only recently released from years of detention, entered the conference room and participated, making also a brief address to the group. Mrs. Chester Bowles, wife of the American ambassador to India, was present at this time.

In the afternoon, participants and observers took a bus to Rajghat, the national shrine where Gandhi's body was cremated the day after his assassination. They walked around the stone marker three times and then shared in the weekly, Friday afternoon prayer meeting. Then they were taken to the nearby Gandhi Museum where they visited its exhibits and watched a short film on the life of Gandhi.

Shri G. Ramachandran, M.P.

WE HAVE BEEN CAREFULLY SELECTING the treasures of thought from the cores of our different religions to prove that they all stand for nonviolence and peace. At the same time, we have confessed to each other that there is a big gap between the ideal and the conduct of the votaries of our religions. We have also stressed again and again that our religions must come into life and face up to the realities, the problems, and the challenges which surround us and not simply sit at the mountain top. It is at this point that Mahatma Gandhi comes to us like a revelation. He demonstrated in his life and work that it is possible for human beings to close the gap between the ideal and the practical. To innumerable requests made to him for a message, his invariable answer was: "My life is my message." This quotation from him is now inscribed beneath his busts, statues, and portraits. In the International Gandhi Centenary Exhibition which we are planning for 1969 here in Delhi, the central court will be called, "My life is my message."

Gandhi once said: "I have met many religious men in my life who were politicians in disguise, but I who appear to be a politician am really at heart a man of religion." He said this half jocularly and half seriously, but for us there is a world of meaning in this. Gandhi was above all a man of religion. Millions of us would perhaps have turned away from religion but for him. And he proved that religion, properly understood, could become a tremendous revolutionary force for changing life into something better, nobler, and greater.

Gandhi insisted that religion must be lived and not preached. Preaching creates the illusion of doing without doing. He challenged the missionaries of every religion, including Hindus, that the only way to spread their religion was through example and living. And yet, what an almighty amount of preaching goes on in the world without effecting inner change in mankind! If millions of people in India followed Gandhi, step by step through many long years, in three great nonviolent revolutions, it was because he set the example and lived the revolutions himself, finally paying the last price a man can for his convictions. He was shot dead by a fanatic Hindu who thought he was sacrificing Hindu interests in favor of the interests of the Muslims of India.

Gandhi was a man of few words and yet, if we were to collect all that he said and wrote, we would perhaps have a greater number of volumes than come from any other world leader. The government of India is now collecting all he said and wrote and this is expected to run into nearly fifty volumes. We must remember, however, that every word Gandhi spoke or wrote was related to something he was doing in terms of human service or for the liberation of man. There are no other two words which occurred more often in his utterances and writings than do truth and nonviolence. These two words he kept in front of him all the time. If I were asked what was the most significant thing about Gandhi, I would say, action. This came to him from the Gītā. Inaction was the negation of truth and nonviolence. Truth and nonviolence must act here and now in the face of every situation. This was the supreme teaching of the Gītā and this was the core of Gandhi's life. To turn away from action in the face of a moral challenge meant committing spiritual suicide. No words, no explanations, no excuses were good enough to explain away inaction. Not nonviolence, therefore, but action came first with Gandhi. Nonviolence was, however, the corollary to action. In other words, action and nonviolence became integrated into one process. I am not convinced that nonviolence came to Gandhi from the Gītā, but action did. Nonviolence came from the Buddha and the Christ and even more from the inescapable needs of the situations in which Gandhi lived, worked, and grew. Gandhi discovered the potency of collective, nonviolent action in the terrible crucible of South Africa where he faced an unparalleled situation in which every hole to freedom was plugged by a government armed to the teeth, not only with weapons but with a perverted and terrible philosophy of cruelty and suppression. Even the thought of a revolt was punishable under the law. It was there that Mahatma Gandhi discovered *satyagraha*, the greatest weapon in the arsenal of man, because it was the weapon with which the physically weakest could fight the physically strongest with a sporting chance of success. Here was a breakthrough in history; previously, and for many centuries, the physically stronger had subjugated the physically weaker. After Gandhi, this was no longer an imperative of history.

If the physically weak must fight the physically strong, the weapon had to be a moral weapon. A moral weapon could be molded only on the anvil of the human spirit. Gandhi discovered not only the incalculable power of the human soul, but the possibility of linking that power to a vast collective process. It was a greater and earlier discovery than the discovery of atomic power. In *satyagraha* we have the ultimate in spiritual power. If Gandhi had not been a man of religion, there would have been no such discovery by him and for mankind. Certainly there would not have been the application of this collective power of the human soul, in a chain reaction process for the liberation of India from British rule, and equally for the liberation of the mind of man from violence and hatred.

Gandhi's God was a revolutionary God leading man from one great destiny to another. There was nothing static about this God. For Gandhi, God alone was the captain of mankind. He had discovered this captain in South Africa and thereafter stuck to him with all the strength of his soul. Even as Gandhi dropped down dead with the bullets of his assassin in his chest, the words that he uttered with his last breath were, "O my God." Gandhi looked upon death as a fulfillment of life and not as an alienation from life. When once there was famine and hunger in Orissa and people were dying by the thousands, he uttered the revolutionary doctrine: "God Himself can today appear before the hungry only in the form of food and work." This utterance of his has entered into the songs of the revolutionaries of India. Even the violent revolutionaries of India look upon Gandhi as a comrade to be loved and respected, because he too was a revolutionary, even if a nonviolent revolutionary.

Let us now consider how far Gandhi was relevant as a religious force for peace. Conflicts and wars arise because there is wrong to be righted, freedom to be secured and defended, and injustice to be remedied. Through uncounted centuries, these tasks were attempted through violent means. But throughout history, violence has led to counterviolence, until ultimately we have today two tremendous and vast systems and patterns of life, each armed with incalculable powers of destruction, confronting each other. Gandhi knew that this escalation of violence was inherent in meeting violence with violence. He also did not run away from the need to right wrongs, defend freedom, and remedy injustice. The arithmetic of this complex proposition pointed to the need for an alternative to violent force.

Gandhi discovered this alternative in *satyagraha* (nonviolence). The discovery of *satyagraha* was the historic necessity of the twentieth century if mankind was to survive at all. We must now notice that violence has always stemmed from the negation of spirituality and nonviolence has equally always stemmed from ethical and spiritual conditions. The harnessing of nonviolence on a commensurate scale was what Gandhi accomplished in South Africa and later in India. His watchwords were "the purification of politics, the moralizing of economics, [and] fighting evil without hating or harming the evil doer." When the battle for Indian freedom ended, and India and England parted company, the gaining of independence was more like a reconciliation than a separation made in anger or hate. If it were possible to win the freedom for India from the British Empire through nonviolence, the possibility is now open in history to win the freedom of mankind from injustice everywhere. We must now admit the possibility of substituting nonviolent collective action for militarism. Gandhi showed the way up to a point. We must now advance further from that point towards world peace. The way is long, but it is open.

Gandhi once said that, if anybody thought religion and politics have nothing to do with each other, then they did not understand either politics or religion. For Gandhi, life was total and integrated. There were no watertight compartments in life. Religion and daily life must come together in every sphere of activity. Religion cannot go one way and politics another.

The fascinating story of how Gandhi has left for us the picture of total and integrated redemption of life is a big chapter by itself.

7. ✍ THE ROLE OF RELIGION IN BUILDING WORLD PEACE

It was the hope of the planners of the Symposium that consideration would be given to what organized religious groups and leaders have already been doing for world peace. Accordingly the seventh session was devoted to a discussion on "The Role of Religion in Building World Peace." Shri U. N. Dhebar was to have been chairman, but he was ill and Mr. Le Roy Anderson agreed to take the chair. Five speakers were heard, after which there was discussion. The chairman's introduction which Shri Dhebar was to have given is included in this compendium.

Ralph David Abernathy

I tremble when I think of the weak men of religion in the second half of the twentieth century who have not the will, understanding, or courage necessary to speak with authority to the political powers. They also do not have the ability to tear down the evil systems of hate, injustice, and inequality so that peace will come to our world—not an uneasy peace, maintained by sword and through fear, but peace which comes only through love, which is *agape*, understanding goodwill towards all men.

For the last 15 years I have given my all in what I consider the struggle for peace in the United States. The movement of which I am a part is best known as the civil rights struggle. It is a revolution of the American Negroes taking place in the United States to secure Negroes their rights guaranteed first by God, our creator, and then by the United States Constitution. For the past fifteen years it has been my task and responsibility to be the vice-president-treasurer of the Southern Christian Leadership Conference and closest associate of Dr. Martin Luther King, Jr., and coleader of the most significant nonviolent movement to take place in the world since Mahatma Gandhi freed a whole nation from colonial exploitation and domination here in this sacred land of India. We have marched the streets side by side and twenty-two times we have been thrown into jail and forced to serve sentences because we refused to obey unjust laws and abide by restrictions imposed upon us solely because of the color of our skin. Martin Luther King and I are known in America as the "civil rights twins" and also as perennial jail mates.

What Martin Luther King and I are trying to do may be called a civil rights movement, but I would rather call it a revolution. It is a revolution in the truest sense of the word for it is a nonviolent revolution. It has brought change without destroying the opposition, and its goal is not to destroy the oppressors but rather to change the evil system and hopefully to change the perpetuators of that system which denies civil rights in the process. Ours is a movement for peace. There cannot be world peace until all of God's children are free and are privileged to enjoy the blessings and goodness of the land. The Negroes' problems cannot be solved until the problems in Vietnam, the Middle East, India, Africa, and all other parts of the world are solved. For that great preacher, John Donne, was correct when he wrote that:

> no man is an island, entire of itself; every man is a piece of the continent, a part of the main; if a clod be washed away by the sea, Europe is the less. . . . Any man's death diminishes me, for I am involved in mankind. . . . And therefore never send to know for whom the bell tolls; it tolls for thee.

Let me emphasize a few of the demands that religion must make in its quest to build world peace. The first is nonviolence. We must put an end to war. The magnificent words of that Negro spiritual, "Ain't Gonna Study War No More," must not be sung only in every nation and in every tongue, but it must become a way of life for all the peoples of the world. The problems facing civilized nations today must be solved around the conference table through the agency of the United Nations. The voice of North Vietnam must be heard with the voice of South Vietnam in the councils of the nations of the world. The People's Republic of China is a fact of history and it must no longer be ignored, but it must be admitted to the United Nations so that its voice will be heard with that of Nationalist China. Then we can get on the road to resolve our differences as nations and peoples.

With vast technological and scientific advancements coupled with the clashing of ideologies, no nation can win a war today. It must be coexistence or nonexistence. The day must soon come when men will beat their swords into ploughshares, their spears into pruning hooks, and study war no more. A great priest and teacher said: "Not by might, not by power, but by my spirit sayeth the Lord of Hosts." You may call it whatever you choose, but I call it God. I have seen his hand move in history. I saw it the other day in Rome as I stood amidst the ruins of the Colosseum and lifted my eyes toward the old city of Rome and the decayed palaces where the mighty emperors once lived and ruled without regard for the worth and dignity of the human personality. I saw that hand of God as it moved through time and history and swept into oblivion the most powerful empire of the ancient world. I saw that hand, the hand of God, as Rome burned while Nero fiddled. That same hand is writing on the wall today. Religionists, if you can't read it, then let me read it for you. It writes: "Be not deceived, for God is not mocked, for whatsoever a man soweth, that he shall also reap."

There is another voice I hear today. It comes from an ancient teacher also, a mighty prophet, the lowly Nazarene. You may just call him Jesus, but I call him a bright light, hope, love, the way, the door, the bread of life, my rock, my fortress, and my God. Yes, Jesus is his name. He says: "Love your enemies, bless them that curse you and pray for them that despitefully use you." He says to every potential Peter: "Put down thy sword, for he that fighteth by the sword shall perish by the sword." So I know that violence is not the way. It is immoral and it is impractical. I have seen violence fail on the streets of Birmingham, Alabama, and in the swamps of Mississippi. Police Chief Bull Connor with all of his police force, guns, and ammunition was forced to stand helpless before the nonviolent army which was armed only with soul force. Through nonviolence, we started a fire that the water hoses could not put out. Nonviolence is the only way to build a permanent and lasting peace. Let us proclaim this truth, each of us in our own way and through our own religion.

If there is to be world peace, then the forces of religion must insist upon the dignity and worth of all human personality. We are all God's children. Let me quote my dearest friend, Martin Luther King, Jr.: "Every man is important in the sight of God—all the way from a bass black to a treble white, we are all significant on God's keyboard."

God is not interested in black men alone. He is not inter-

ested in white men only, nor is he interested only in brown or
yellow men. God is interested in all men, white and black,
brown and yellow. There is only one God. If he is the
father of all of us, then we are, therefore, all brothers. That is
why we sing in the freedom movement: "We shall overcome
some day; deep in our hearts we do believe; we shall overcome
some day." Yes, black and white believe that we shall overcome. Many people are becoming frustrated, hopeless, and
disillusioned. Because of the slow pace we are making in the
direction of human rights and individual freedom, they are
turning aside to false detour signs such as black power,
separatism, and uprisings in cities (the so-called riots). Our
road to world peace does not lead through these. We will not
win through black power, white power, and not even through
"green power." But we will win only through the power of
God.

In my country, we read these words in the Declaration of
Independence:

> We hold these truths to be self-evident, that all men are
> created equal and they are endowed by their Creator, with
> certain inalienable rights, among these are life wants and the
> pursuit of happiness. . . .

We also read in the Bible: "Out of one blood, God created
all nations to dwell upon the face of the Earth." Science is
doing its job. Technology is doing its job very well, but it is
sad to say that religions with all their dogmas, creeds, hymns,
and anthems are lagging far behind. Science and technology
have made our world a neighborhood. This is a fact. But religions have failed to make of our world a brotherhood. They
tell us that we shall soon be on the moon, yet we have not
learned how to live here on the earth. Time is running out
and unless you and I inject new dimensions into the veins of
our civilization, then it shall only become trash and ruin on
the junk piles of time and eternity. "Be not deceived, for

God is not mocked, for whatsoever a man soweth, that shall he also reap." These words are of great significance and they hold great truths. There will not be world peace until Jew and Gentile, Catholic and Protestant, Hindu and Muslim, Buddhist and Jain, believer and nonbeliever, are all recognized, treated, and respected as God's children.

The religions of the world must insist upon a more equal distribution of wealth in the world. No civilization can survive very long if it denies necessities to the masses only to give luxuries to the classes. How long do we think we can get by with two-thirds of the peoples of the world going to bed hungry each and every night, living without adequate clothing and shelter, with little or no medical and dental care, while the rest of the world feasts sumptuously like rich Dives and will not give even the crumbs that fall from the table to the millions of poor Lazaruses. Remember, this is my father's word and David has well said: "The earth is the Lord's, the fullness thereof, the world and they that dwell therein." There is plenty of food, clothing, and shelter to spare in the world for all of God's children. The great need is a more equal distribution of these goods.

It is our job to use these means: nonviolent resistance, respect for the worth and dignity of all human personality, and a more equal distribution of the world's wealth. Even other means may be necessary to bring about peace in our world in our time. As prophets, we must stand in the courts of the nations of the world and echo what sayeth the Lord:

> For the spirit of the Lord is upon us, because He has sent us to preach the Gospel to the poor. He has anointed us to heal the broken hearted, to free the captives, to set at liberty them that are bruised, and to proclaim the acceptable year of the Lord.

To quote another great poet whose lines have been set to music and sung often in our Baptist churches:

Once to every man and nation
Comes the moment to decide,
In the strife of truth with falsehood,
For the good or evil side,
Then it is the brave man chooses,
While the coward stands aside,
Till the multitude make virtue
Of the faith they have denied.

For my stand, I have seen my earthly possessions, including automobile and home, sold at public auction, I have been sued for three million dollars—more money than I, my wife, my children, and my grandchildren will make in our lifetimes. I have been beaten, arrested, and thrown into jail twenty-two times. I, like the apostle Paul, bear on my body the bruises and marks of a soldier of the cross. I have been forced to stand over the ruins of my church that was dynamited and over the rubbish of my home that was bombed—a home where my wife and child barely escaped death. Many of my colleagues have given their lives in the struggle, and I have had the sad and awesome responsibility of preaching their funerals. But I will not lose faith and I will not turn back. I will not turn back, for world opinion is on our side. God is on our side, you are on our side, and we are on our own side. We will have peace in the world, if we as religionists will not become so busy and preoccupied with the rituals and ceremonies as did the priest and the Levite, so that we may not administer to the needs of the men on the Jericho road. Let us get down in the gutter with humanity, as did the Samaritan, and administer to the needs of the peoples of the world. This will take our religion beyond the four walls of synagogue, church, and mosque. We must keep moving until all of God's children—black, white, brown, and yellow, rich and poor, believer and nonbeliever, can stand up and say: "Free at last, free at last, thanks, God Almighty, we are free at last." Then, and only then, will we have peace in the world.

Archbishop Angelo Fernandes

JUST AS THERE is the science of pure mathematics and applied mathematics, so the challenges of today seem to call for greater emphasis on "applied religion" as a manifestation of union with God and eternal principles.

I do not need to stress, therefore, the background thinking of Christ and his church, the vision, motivation, and dynamism of Christianity itself for justice and peace in the interest of a true brotherhood of man under the fatherhood of God. Let me rather share with you briefly the aims, objectives, and initial efforts made by the International Vatican Justice and Peace Commission.

The Second Vatican Council was a mighty corporate effort, initiated by Pope John XXIII. It was continued by Pope Paul VI, along with the 3,000 Catholic bishops of the entire world and the assistance of the flock from everywhere. It has given to the church and the world the guidelines of an "applied Christianity" for the world of today, age-old truths and structures presented afresh in an increasingly relevant manner for the challenges of the world of today.

One document in particular concerned itself with international questions—the fostering of peace and the promotion of the community of nations. This is well worth study and reflection by all interested in promoting the cause of justice and peace.

Inasmuch as the immensity of the hardships which still inflict the greater part of mankind today constitute one of the principal reasons militating against peace, the council thought it opportune that an organism of the universal church be set up in order that both the justice and love of Christ towards the poor be developed everywhere. The role of the organism is to stimulate progress in needy regions and international social justice.

When Pope Paul VI set up the Justice and Peace Commission for this purpose, he said its general aim would be:

> . . . to arouse the whole People of God to a full awareness of its mission at the present time. On the one hand it would promote the progress of needy countries and encourage social justice between nations, and on the other hand it would help the less developed nations to work themselves towards their own development.

In the spring of 1967, the Holy Father issued a document on the development of peoples, in which he again stressed that the Commission was charged:

> . . . to bring to the whole of God's people the full knowledge of the part expected of them at the present time, so as to further the progress of poorer peoples, to encourage social justice among nations, to offer to less-developed nations the means whereby they can further their own progress. . . . Its name, which is also its program, is Justice and Peace. . . . We think that this can and should bring together men of good will with our Catholic sons and our Christian brothers. So it is to all that we address this solemn appeal for concrete action towards man's complete development and the development of all mankind.

The Commission held its first meeting in April 1967, and as a result of its deliberations issued a statement outlining its program. This stressed the need to operate at two different levels and at two different speeds. It must seek to elaborate the doctrine of the Pope's document and work on the application of its teaching to the concrete realities of the world today.

The division corresponds to the two different scales of time. The world is in a desperate crisis. The gap between developed and developing nations increases as the wealth of the rich grows steadily and the needy are threatened with stagnation or worse. The risk of famine grows each year. This action must consist in developed and developing nations joining as equal partners in the building of a more just and peaceful world, without the glaring inequalities which now exist.

Perhaps the chief reason for these inequalities is that most men still lack any final loyalty to the whole family of man. They are divided by all kinds of divisions and separations—tribalistic, nationalistic, racial. These cannot be eliminated from one day to the next. The effort demands long-term education in the fundamental principles of justice and peace, which the commission will also seek to promote.

The Commission suggested that bishops' conferences be held in every land; that all concerned with education should be encouraged to include the teaching of international social justice in the curricula of colleges, theological schools, universities, and all institutions of learning; that religious instruction in general should emphasize the discussion of world justice; that, where possible, this should be done ecumenically and with all men of goodwill, so that eventually there would be an accepted program of worldwide development and justice.

The Commission also chose some priority programs which were in keeping with the priorities of *Populorum Progressio,* where the Pope singled out two issues of action:

> The flow of resources from rich to poor (the world tax, the world fund, the question of poor nations debt burden) and the inequalities in the organization of world trade. These issues deserve priority treatment because both increase immediately the resources available for all forms of desirable development and because they test the sincerity of the rich nations.

Since the first meeting of the Commission, activities of members, consultors, and the Central Secretariat in Rome have been largely centered on the formation of national commissions in developing and developed countries.

On the practical plane, therefore, the Commission strives to achieve its purpose by stimulating all organizations within the church in all parts of the world to propagate the ideas of social justice and peace enshrined in *Populorum Progressio.* It also inspires the local church in every country to play its part in promoting development and in promoting economic cooperation and equitable trade for developing countries by pressure of public opinion. Many such commissions have since been formed in Latin America, Africa, Asia, Western Europe, and North America.

The second meeting of the Commission in October 1967 studied in greater depth some of the points outlined above. It has since instituted permanent committees for deepening the study of the church's teaching with regard to development of economic cooperation and trade in the light of this teaching; the role of the church in developing nations; the role of the church in developed nations; and the issues of peace, especially the longer term of the building of the structures of the new world. In addition, a committee has been established on development, family, and population.

In view of the UNCTAD meeting in New Delhi, special attention was given to the matter of economic cooperation. Mr. K. B. Lall, commerce secretary of the government of India, who addressed the Commission immediately after the Algiers meeting, said that those in the lands of the poor who were trying to break the thraldom of poverty were grateful to the Holy Father for his support. He said: "Feeling for the poor has always been one of the pillars of the Catholic Church. But the Holy Father has applied the traditional teaching to the problems of the day." This was shown, he went on, by the encyclical, by his visit to Bombay, by his visit to the United Nations, and also by the support extended to India when the country was facing two years of drought—support which "enabled us to live through one of the most difficult periods of our history." He finally conveyed through the Commission his gratitude to the Holy Father.

In December 1967, under the auspices of the Indian Social Institute, a seminar on these topics was held in New Delhi with international participation.

Even more significant perhaps has been the Brussels meeting of December 1967. Under the auspices of the Christian Churches of the Atlantic Region, on the premises of the European Economic Community, and with the cooperation of governmental leaders, these subjects were discussed with a view to creating a better climate in the world and particularly for the UNCTAD meeting in New Delhi.

An ecumenical venture of epoch-making importance is planned for April 1968 in Lebanon with Dr. Jan Tinbergen, Lady Jackson, and other such personalities already committed to participation. This is being held under the joint auspices of the World Council of Churches and the Justice and Peace Commission.

Would it not be a good idea if, in order to make the force of every religion more relevant in the world of today, each religion which is not already doing so made an effort to select from its treasures, the concepts, examples, and perhaps techniques that would specifically help the key problem of building a better world in and through the field of economic cooperation? This should be understood as a common human endeavor that each man and all mankind may have the opportunity for integrated human development.

If each religion's ideas on justice, development, and peace were put between book covers—as has been done by the Catholic church in recent years through documents like *Mater et Magistra, Pacem in Terris, The Church in the Modern World*, and *Populorum Progressio*—that might provide the basis for common action in the years ahead.

Even before this is done, our common concern about the

present world situation, the desire for peace and brotherhood on the part of people everywhere, and the spirit of hope, born of the determination to try to create the structures for world justice and peace, should be given expression everywhere and broadcast to the ends of the earth through the use of the media of social communication. This public relations endeavor might help to create the climate that would induce world leaders to work effectively along the lines of human solidarity and love triumphing over fear and hate.

The ecumenical meeting of specialists is being asked to make program proposals to the sponsoring bodies in order to lay the groundwork for ecumenical collaboration in promoting world justice, development, and peace in the coming years.

There is no reason why the scope of such meetings should not be broadened in the years ahead to bring together specialists from all religions, all men of goodwill everywhere concerned to make their contribution towards the building of a better world.

Inasmuch as world justice and peace depend ultimately on personal peace in each man and in families, a simultaneous movement around the world is taking place in all Christian communities seeking to make Sunday and weekday worship ever more meaningful, to tighten the bonds between the love of God and the concrete manifestation of that love for one's neighbor in personal and corporate fashion. The effort is meant to reach out to the base, the flock, and not only to the pastors and leaders, so that in a spirit of teamwork all within the church and others with them may reach out in ever-widening circles towards the attainment of the goals of justice and peace.

This is the spirit of the message of His Holiness, Pope Paul VI, when he exhorted all men of goodwill to celebrate the first day of the year throughout the world as the Day of Peace. He said:

It is our desire that this commemoration be repeated every year as a hope and as a promise that the beginning of the calendar, which measures and outlines the path of human life in time, that peace with its just and beneficent equilibrium may dominate the development of events to come and guide the ship of civilization through the inescapable storms of history to the harbor of its highest destiny.

Pope Paul composed a prayer for use on New Year's Day and this is its final paragraph:

Remember, O Father of mercy, all those who struggle, suffer, and die to bring forth a world of closer brotherhood. May your kingdom of justice, of peace, and of love come to men of every race and every tongue. And may the earth be filled with your glory!

Msgr. Edward G. Murray

EACH ONE OF US speaks necessarily from within his own tradition and hence much of what I have to say is colored by the fact that I speak as a monotheist, a Christian, and a Westerner. Yet I trust that what I say will find its echo in great measure among all of us.

Peace is after all too important an objective to be left only to statesmen or politicians. It is both an end that we seek, and a dimension within which we hope that the world of the future may live in totally accustomed fashion.

Face to face with the awesome possibilities of nuclear warfare, a great leader for peace, Norman Cousins, entitled one of his books *Who Speaks for Man?* It is our belief that even in the secular state and secular society, nothing speaks more eloquently for man than the imperatives of religious ethics. These spring from belief in a pattern of order which imposes itself as a transcendent duty for mankind.

We have recognized in this Symposium the many forces that tend to make man aggressive. They range from greed and pride to the instinctive functioning of the adrenal glands. Yet we are agreed that none of these is beyond the free control of man, if he is supremely motivated to peace.

Our own personal and historical experience tells us that, when we need to be motivated toward those things which are against the clamor of our own egos, it is the insistent voice of religious conscience that leads us to do the good that must be done. We may call it our religion, our ideology, our mystique, or our value pattern. But by whatsoever name, we know that we share a sense of value above all particular, immediate, and personal values. This highest value of ours, in every tradition, is a force that motivates toward peace. Every paper read in this Symposium, every comment made, bears its own testimony to the existence of this highest order of truth to which we feel obedience.

In the United States, we are one people who come from backgrounds of great cultural diversity. It is clear to us, however, and we hope that it is clear to those who know our country, that we share a common sense of values in the moral-political order which we call the Judeo-Christian ethic.

It is by reason of this that in the United States the largest religious groups—Protestant, Catholic, Orthodox, and Jewish —find themselves at one in regard to most of the moral questions which trouble us. It was not difficult for us to recognize the need to speak and work together relative to the grave problems of racial injustice. We find ourselves likewise sharing common goals as we work for peace—that peace which is the fruit of justice, as our common scriptures commend to us. We believe still in our own special faiths, but we unite in this communal concern. This is why the U.S. Inter-Religious Committee on Peace speaks with one voice.

In both of these fields of racial harmony and of international peace, we Americans have undertaken not so much to move our government as to move those members of our society who pay heed to us as religious teachers and leaders. It is the voice of the people which ultimately is heard, and the power of the government does not avail against the voice of the people when it has spoken. Therefore, each of our religious bodies has repeatedly undertaken to speak to the American people relative to the imperatives of peace, confident that, as we underline the religious dimensions of peace, every other value that might lead to war will be seen rather as a disvalue. One of our great philosophers, William James, has said that mankind needs something which will be the moral equivalent of war—something that will arouse men to the excitement of great loyalty in a common effort and will make sacrifice seem acceptable because undertaken for a great cause.

We have pointed out that our warfare can be tremendously exciting if directed against poverty, ignorance, discrimination, and disease. We are happy that so many of our young Americans in particular have channeled their altruism and their religious concept of the brotherhood of man into service for others both at home and abroad.

The Synagogue Council of America, speaking for all the groups within United States religious Judaism, issued the following statement last year:

A decisive contribution of Judaism to the morality of international affairs is the affirmation that nations like individuals must be guided in their actions by justice and morality. Nations like individuals cannot escape God's judgment for "He will judge the Universe with justice and nations with righteousness." Because nations are composed of individuals, it is ultimately the individual who must assume moral responsibility and moral judgment in the affairs of his country.

Continuing to one of the major preoccupations in the quest for peace, the Synagogue Council stated:

No one course of action in this complicated situation [in Vietnam] can clearly solve the moral dilemma in which we find ourselves. The U.S. commitment to the Government of South Vietnam has created a moral responsibility which we cannot ignore in our quest for peace. Yet having searched our conscience, we have come to the conclusion that peace and the cessation of hostilities must remain our major objective.

The General Board of the National Council of the Churches of Christ in America, representing Protestant and Orthodox groups, has issued an important statement of policy, precipitated by the Southeast Asia conflict, but with the following general principle:

We call upon Christians in the United States to do these things.

1. The first thing we must do, and perhaps the most difficult and most important, is to maintain our spiritual and ethical sensitivity and keep before us our awareness of the imperatives of the Christian Gospel. In wartime, this is often the first casualty. These imperatives are all known for they are clearly written in the New Testament, "Love your enemies, and pray for those who persecute you. . . . If your enemy is hungry feed him, . . . And He made from one every nation of man to live on all the face of the earth. . . . Do not be conformed to the world, but be transformed by the renewal of your mind. . . . Do not be overcome by evil, but overcome evil with good!"

2. Let peacemaking be the priority of our Christian witness so that we may be truly children of God in these difficult times.

3. Support the efforts of the National Council of Churches in an approach to the World Council of Churches and Pope Paul VI in a common attempt to mobilize the worldwide Christian community in support of a just alternative to war.

For the Catholic position, we have words of the Second Vatican Council which plead for peace. Above all we have words of the great advocate of peace, Pope Paul VI. His New Year's 1968 message calls for a day of peace and prayers for peace at the beginning of each year. He addressed the first part of the New Year's message to "all men of good will, including governments, international organizations, religious institutions, and particularly youth whose insight regarding the new paths of civilization is more lively." The second part was addressed to the bishops and faithful of the Catholic church.

In the first part, Pope Paul VI declared that international organizations that have been created to foster international respect, collaboration, and development must be supported by all, become better known, and be provided with authority and the means fit for their great mission.

We remember that this is the pope who, after coming to India to speak the words of peace and love, went before the United Nations at the invitation of the nations of the world and stated in impassioned eloquence: "War no more! War never, never again!" He pleaded likewise that the United Nations accept every nation in the world as a member.

The Pope went on in his message to warn that:

> peace cannot be founded on false and flimsy words which are welcomed because they answer to the deep, genuine aspirations of humanity, but which can also serve—and unfortunately have sometimes served—to hide the lack of a true spirit and of real intention for peace . . . there is no true peace unless the foundations of peace are respected. . . . These foundations are four: *Within* each nation, liberty. *Among* nations they are sincerity, justice, and love.

Without these foundations, no peace will exist, but there will be an unceasing and irrepressible growth of revolt and war.

In the second portion of his talk the Pope said that he addresses himself constantly to the need for peace, not out of a facile habit, but by reason of the tremendous urgency of the present situation. He spoke of "intimations of terrible events which may prove catastrophic for entire nations and perhaps even for a great part of manhood. Peace is the only true direction of human progress."

The task of bringing these words to fulfillment will not be easy. We must approach it in the spirit of Paul of Tarsus who undertook his ministry "in great endurance, in afflictions, in hardships, in straits, in scourgings, in imprisonments, in riots, in fatigues, in sleepless nights, in fastings, in integrity, in knowledge, in long-suffering, in kindness, in the gifts of the Holy Spirit, in unaffected love, in the preaching of the truth, in the power that comes from God." Then peace will be ours.

Rev. Riri Nakayama

As an old and humble Buddhist worker in Tokyo, I boldly sit here because of my earnest desire to avoid the nuclear war which might annihilate mankind at the culminant escalation of the Vietnamese war. May I refer to my stand first, as a Japanese Buddhist clergyman of the Mahāyāna school? Buddhism is said to be a peaceful religion and it is rightly said. History shows that in its 2,500 years of silent propagation, not a drop of blood has ever been shed in its name.

Gautama Buddha is often called the prince of peace. Buddhism speaks of peace rather than happiness, the reason being that peace is the foundation for happiness. I understand that life is peaceful when one is always with this hope. Hope requires time. Therefore, belief in one's immortality is the source of hope that leads one to peace. The Buddhist way of life is always accompanied by self-introspection for eternity.

Self means invisible self, the master of the physical body. The physical body changes with death, but the invisible self defies changes. One's self is immortal.

The Sukhavati Vyuna Sūtra suggests a paradise where people realize immortality of their own selves according to the teaching of Amita Buddha. *Amita* in the Sanskrit language means immortality. Amita Buddha means the enlightened one who realizes his own immortality. Hence Sukhavati Vyuna Sūtra is translated by Chinese monks as the Sutra of Immortality Preachings.

When one realizes the immortality of one's own invisible self, one can embrace bright hope in any walk of life. To keep many precepts, to practice Zen contemplation, to pray by chanting *sūtras* or chanting the name of Amita Buddha or Saddharma Pundarīka Sūtra are diverse methods of Buddhism for the realization of the immortality of oneself. One cannot but be peaceful when one realizes his own immortality. Hence, Buddhism is a peaceful religion. The world religions must be common in this point.

"Man is mortal" is an iron maxim from time unknown. Man, however, does not wish to be mortal. Man obeys his life's destiny with discontent and abandonment which does not make man peaceful. Hence uneasiness and irritation are consummated as intolerance and dichotomization.

Intolerance is to see only one's own side and forget or neglect to see the point of view of others. Why do communist countries force other countries to follow communism and capitalistic nations force others to become capitalistic nations? Enforcing interference is to be restrained.

Toleration is a virtue. Buddhism is said to be a religion of toleration. However, the use of the word "toleration" is not appropriate for Buddhism because toleration itself connotes superiority. One tolerates and the other is tolerated. In Buddhism it is not toleration, but understanding and a feeling of oneness. Here is peace.

The concept of dichotomization should be analyzed as one of the basic concepts of world conflict. That is to say, all the views, thoughts, ideas, and ways of life are dualistic. It may be said that modern culture is the culture of conflicts of sets of pairs. The Buddhist nondualistic way of teaching is that there is no eternity without the present, or the now-moment; now is the eternal present; eternity and the present cannot be divided.

East and West are only conceptual; in reality, there is no East or West, just contrast. The Buddhist enlightenment is the realization of oneness of life originated from the realization of one's immortality. It teaches the illusions of separateness. It teaches oneness. This is the foundation for peace. The fundamental role of religionists in building world peace is to share their belief of immortality of oneself, or oneness of life, or other sacred gospels of their respective religions, with people without faith. This will eliminate their hidden uneasiness and discontentment which might develop into a sinister force to be used against the peace and harmony of mankind.

At this critical time when a push-button war might finish the whole of humanity with its civilization attained by the culminated effort of long centuries, we religionists must hurry to our urgent role in building world peace. We are obliged to act energetically to demand a ceasefire by approaching the political leaders of both camps, right and left, democratic and communistic.

Our hearty appeal for peace in this International Inter-Religious Symposium will be sure to influence many peoples who hear of it. However, political leaders of both camps will not readily listen to our plea while the keys for world peace or world war are kept in their hands.

Last summer, after one week's visit to Saigon, I attended the 13th World Congress of the World Federalists in Oslo to help expedite the realization of a world federation, world law, and one world. This ideal was referred to at the inaugural address by Dr. Zakir Husain, President of India, and Shri R. R. Diwakar, chairman of our Symposium.

The Oslo Congress was filled with high-toned speeches expressing anxiety for the fate of humankind. There was, however, no actual influence on matter-of-fact politicians of both camps.

After the Oslo Congress, I visited the Vatican to have an interview with His Holiness, Pope Paul VI, to discuss the Vietnamese issue. I extended my trip to North and South America. I stayed in Washington and New York City for several weeks to sound out ideas on ceasefire in Vietnam with the state department, senators and congressmen, both doves and hawks. I listened to the debates in the United Nations General Assembly. It might be no exaggeration to say that few delegations from the 122 member nations went to the rostrum without referring to the unhappy and dangerous situation in Vietnam. But speakers were content just to talk. There was no solution.

It is my sad impression that the United States of America and the U.S.S.R. or continental China would not hesitate to start a war of human annihilation if circumstances affect their respective national prestige.

Our unique duty as world religionists is to play the role of mediators among the politicians, the military, and peoples of both camps who are on edge.

I make a sincere suggestion that this International Inter-Religious Symposium on Peace encourage the founding of inter-religious committees on peace in the respective countries which can cooperate with each other to avoid human crisis from the standpoint of common religious ideals. They may result in a world inter-religious organization on peace which could help the present United Nations Organization.

Our role as representatives of world religions at present is, therefore, to persuade both camps to become enlightened to humanism, freed from old-fashioned and cursed intolerance, and never to resort to military force for the promulgation of their political ideologies. This is the apparent cause of world war, either cold or hot.

It is ironic to see both camps indulge in desperate struggles, ready to set off a nuclear war of human annihilation, which both ideologies—Marxism and democracy—started for the cause of humanity.

The militant methods, however, were frequently used throughout the history of religions for their own aggrandizement. Hence we find such phrases as "religion for too many centuries has been the cause of hatred and actual war" in the invitation of our Symposium. The wars between religions are now the story of the remote past. Let the modern statesmen of both political camps not follow this out-of-date pattern of religions. With this shameful historical past, we world religionists are all the more qualified for the role of humble mediators between the struggling camps.

May I recall the World Pacifist Meeting in Santiniketan and Sevagram in December 1949, which I attended with two Christian friends from Japan. The meeting was convened by Rajendra Prasad, Jawaharlal Nehru, Shri Horace Alexander, and Shri G. Ramachandran. Now Prasad and Nehru, both of whom were apostles of peace-making, are gone. The world situation, however, has become worse during the succeeding nineteen years. We realize the difficulty of peace-making, but it must be challenged by us religionists of the world who have no ambition, political or economic, except the burning wish for world peace. As a Buddhist delegate from Japan, the only nation in the world that twenty-three years ago experienced the horror of atom bombings, I hope this International Inter-Religious Symposium on Peace will take some practical step for the realization of world peace.

Jambel D. Gomboev

ALLOW ME, on behalf of the Buddhists of the U.S.S.R. and on my own behalf, to convey sincere greetings to the organizing committee and to all participants of this international Symposium.

I, as a Buddhist monk, feel very happy to witness that today, in this hall, representatives of various religions of the world have gathered to exchange views on essential questions of the peace movement all over the world. All mankind is one before religion. Therefore, as our great teacher, Lord Buddha, said, all mankind must live in peace and quiet, to enjoy happiness and prosperity, and to deliver itself from sufferings and misfortunes which are caused by different kinds of evil.

We, representatives of different religions, acknowledge that these propositions are the basis of any religion, irrespective of what religion we profess and what its religious and philosophic dogmas and holy canons are. Suffering of living beings is a common phrase which can be understood by people of any religion. According to Buddha's teaching, the principal mission of religion on earth is to deliver mankind from sufferings of any kind. From age-old history, war was always the source of all disasters and misfortunes for people. Bloodshed and murder, robbery and violence, hypocrisy and lies—these are constant companions of war. Therefore, the great Buddha, whose name became a symbol of peace, always condemned both the instigators and the participants of any crime. War is the worst crime. He called upon kings and czars to abstain from waging wars and to live in peace for the sake of happiness and prosperity in the world.

In his time, the great Buddha, by the power of his teachings, stopped many disastrous wars and presented people with peace. Our present strife-ridden world needs Buddha as never before to establish peace and quiet on the earth. This great mission can and must be performed by us, the representatives of many religions. We must join our efforts and devote our lives to the just and noble struggle for the prevention of world wars, for the cessation of hostilities and nuclear tests, and for full and complete disarmament. I believe that this Symposium, being held in the motherland of the great Buddha and dedicated to the problems of religion and peace, can contribute to establishing peace on earth, to the cessation of American aggression in South Vietnam, and of Israeli aggression in the Middle East. The Buddhists of the Soviet Union cannot keep away when the blood of their brothers in faith is being shed every day on the earth.

The Central Religions Board of Buddhists of the U.S.S.R. has lodged protests many times against aggression in these parts of the world. The Buddhists of the U.S.S.R. have sent a large amount of medicine to South Vietnam to help the people who are the victims of aggression.

We, Buddhist monks in the Soviet Union, in our everyday prayers appeal to our great teacher, Lord Buddha, and call upon the heads of state and government to stop the bloodshed and to put an end to the horrors and sufferings of the people. Our struggle to stop aggression in Vietnam and imperialist aggression in the Middle East is being shared by the whole Soviet people. Every Soviet citizen, whatever religion he follows, who prays to God, in whatever language, and to whatever God it might be, calls on all representatives of this Symposium to raise their voice for the sake of preserving peace, prosperity, and progress on earth.

We have a deep conviction that the great desire of the Soviet Buddhists and of the whole of our country for peace all over the world is being shared unanimously by all the participants of this Symposium. With your permission I will conclude with a prayer asking deliverance for living beings from sufferings and asserting happiness and welfare in the present-day world.

Shri U. N. Dhebar*

THE CHALLENGES to the cause of world peace are many. The consequences of a large-scale breach of peace in the world are likely to be disastrous. The scope of the operation of forces of religion has become increasingly limited. Manipulation by the state of the systems of education, and through it of men's minds in nearly half of the world; developing socio-democratic society overshadowed by an industrial-military complex in about another third; and nearly a third of the world's people living on the borderlines of destitution where the basic cry is for bread—these situations do not offer a very hospitable background to men searching for peace. The exercise in considering the role of religion in building up world peace may in this context *prima facie* appear to be futile.

To think of religion as the only element that can save peace will, of course, be presumptuous. There was perhaps a time centuries back when religion was such a force. The common man is seldom known to have reposed confidence in religion in its whole history to the extent he did in that period. Religion nevertheless continues to be one of the noblest urges of the human soul. It is a pity that its expression is confined to the side currents of history's torrential flow.

There is a misunderstanding which needs to be removed that religion has concerned itself with matters of the other world. We live in a matter-of-fact world and, in a sense, the

* Prepared for delivery. Shri Dhebar became ill and could not be chairman of the session.

world has always been a matter-of-fact world. It would not have cut much ice with the people of the world if Jesus, Buddha, Gandhi, Moses, or Mohammed had thought in unrealistic terms of a world that "should be" but "was not." They thought in terms of correctives, because they realized that the workaday world would be there even after they had left it. They wanted to leave it in better shape than it was when they came on the scene.

The first thing about which this human world would naturally be concerned at a practical level is with its own existence. The questions of stability, progress, and evolution are no doubt important. The question of primary importance is this: Is there a practical answer to war? Since war does not come from a vacuum, but is a resultant factor of a deeper malaise, is there a way out, firstly, for removing the present causes of conflict and, secondly, for preventing others to arise? These two questions need primary consideration. Is there any way to tackle those international conflicts which in the long or short run promise to ripen into shooting wars? Is there any way by which it is possible to order international life so that it does not allow such disputes to arise or, in case they arise, simultaneously to solve them?

I have often wondered if religions of the world can re-create the former faith and fervor in the hearts and minds of the people so as to have concrete effectiveness in a short spell of time. I have already described the massive pattern of the organized social mind the world over.

The first thing that the world wants to know is whether there is a practical alternative to war. Perhaps at some point in history, religions as they were practiced may also have contributed to war. In a vital question of this sort, none can indulge in oversimplification or generalizations. None will dispute the view that religions, whether practiced in the East or the West, the North or the South, have, in a degree, been responsible for what now appears on the surface as the basic reasons which may supply fire to the faggots of human passions.

For instance, can we say in relation to religions in India that men, whatever their faith, have adequately concerned themselves with basic socioeconomic issues leading to the ever-growing pace of human misery until freedom was achieved? Have they, as rational beings, realized that a human being must put a morsel of food in his stomach to give him strength to recite a vedic *mantra* or a hymn from the Bible? Can we say that the mandarins of China, expressing their devotion to the God of compassion or the venerable Buddha, ever bothered two hoots about a similar situation developing there? A few decades back, a little to the west of China, the old Orthodox church was equally unconcerned with the continuous erosion of faith in man and in values it wanted to perpetuate. Similarly, can it be said of the men of religion in the West that they have not tolerated if not abetted, racial discrimination and human exploitation by the colonial powers in the past?

This is not a story of the past. It is a continuing one. What despicable atrocities we saw being committed in India during the last days of the British *raj* in the name of religions! Similarly there is no evidence yet that the racial issue has been taken up by the clergy as a whole, whether in South Africa or in North America. On both sides of Vietnam, human beings, perhaps following the same religion, and their missionaries too, go on emphasizing that the cause in their half of Vietnam is the holiest of the holy. We hear only weak protests against the development of nuclear weapons from stray quarters within the precincts of church, temple, mosque, or monastery in comparison with the consequences involved.

Can leadership in religion, so long as it has not cleared its own mind, expect to be listened to with faith and followed with conviction? After everything is said and done between man and God, the term integrity can only mean fullness of commitment and wholeness of conduct. Under the circumstances, this can be the only appropriate starting point for any effective role religious leadership can play in facing this crisis.

Peace is a term which is variously interpreted. The interpretations range from genuine friendly relationship to the absence of active hostility. At the juncture of human development where we stand, peace in concrete terms cannot be expected to be anything less than the determination to maintain and strengthen the friendliness wherever it exists and a still greater determination to forge conditions that enable friendliness to replace animosity.

In the three areas that threaten world peace, an initiative in leading a dialogue should be made possible. The West/East relationship is the most potent of these areas. Leadership in the religious world can render a significant contribution by initiating efforts at the popular international level in all available forums with a view to influencing a dialogue between Hanoi and Washington, with the hope of awakening the conscience of mankind. There is one great advantage that the predominant urge in the Southeast Asian countries is still nationalism. If not utilized in time, this urge may capitulate finally to the force for expansionism.

In the area of racial discrimination, there should be an unequivocal declaration of the equality of man, from all quarters of the world. In recent history, Gandhi in South Africa and Dr. Martin Luther King, Jr., in the United States can be considered as our beacon lights.

In relation to the production and use of nuclear armaments, there should be an unequivocal demand for the declaration of a complete prohibition thereof. To whatever nationality they may belong, leaders of religions, the world over, should subscribe to this goal wholeheartedly.

The other problems concerning humanity which bear upon the question of peace are there. In a fast-developing situation with science and technology continuously affecting the mind of man, it will be difficult for anyone to comprehend the entire problem in one single grasp. In India, for example, we have especially the problem of poverty.

Whether it is religious, social, economic, or political leadership, the universal mind must be concentrated upon the main task of relieving tensions and forging enduring peace. I can only hope that this Symposium will take us a step forward in that direction.

8. ✍ A WORLD CONFERENCE ON RELIGION AND PEACE

ONE OF THE PRIME PURPOSES of the Symposium was to evaluate the need for a world conference on religion and peace. The eighth and ninth sessions were devoted to this topic. The eighth session was chaired by Prof. M. Mujeeb, vice-chancellor of Jamia Millia Islamia, a university in Delhi. Rabbi André Zaoui led a religious service. Dr. Homer A. Jack then presented a paper on "A World Conference on Religion and Peace: Its Desirability and Feasibility." Discussion followed. The ninth session in the afternoon consisted of two simultaneous group discussions on a world conference, with participants and observers arbitrarily assigned to the groups. The findings of both groups were combined and these were received and approved at the eleventh session.

Homer A. Jack

THIS INTERNATIONAL INTER-RELIGIOUS SYMPOSIUM ON PEACE has so far amply demonstrated that most world religions and many of their leaders and adherents—which means most of mankind—have dreamt of the time when all nations can turn their swords into plowshares and all men can learn war no more. In recent years, and occasionally throughout history, the leaders of some world religions have been impatient with the slow pace of the politicians and statesmen in reaching this goal. Today, in the nuclear age, this goal of world peace is not merely desirable; it is essential, and men of religion know that they must constantly remind statesmen of the primacy and urgency of this goal.

Within the past one hundred years, organized religion has occasionally taken some leadership in the field of international relations and peace. The World Parliament of Religion was held in Chicago during the last decade of the nineteenth century. While this had more of an inter-religious than a peace objective, both values were intertwined in this historic gathering, which had the active participation of Asian religious leaders.

Between the two world wars of this century, there was one persistent, if abortive, effort for a World Conference for International Peace Through Religion. The poignant story of this effort is given in some detail in the published report of the exploratory mission which the Rev. Herschel Halbert and I undertook for the U.S. Inter-Religious Committee on Peace last spring. We discovered by accident some traces of this prewar effort in Japan. The hopes and then the frustrations of this World Conference for International Peace Through Religion are well worth pondering, especially in our more optimistic moments. Although from 1924 to 1938 much time, energy, and money were spent to convene this world conference, and such notable figures as Gandhi and Einstein were in touch with the effort, events caught up with the planners and World War II broke out before the conference could be convened.[1]

Since the end of World War II, the demands for a world

[1] See Appendix B.

gathering of religious leaders for peace have been even more insistent. Some religious leaders have individually called for world peace, sometimes in specific political terms. In the past decade, one need only recall the prophetic utterances against war by the late Martin Buber in Israel, the late Albert Schweitzer in Africa, and the late Pope John XXIII in the Vatican. If their individual voices could have been brought together in the early nineteen sixties, the chorus would have made a great impact upon their followers and, in turn, on world statesmen. This potential was recognized by such American religious leaders as Rabbi Maurice N. Eisendrath and Dr. Dana McLean Greeley who individually and separately almost a decade ago called for a world summit meeting of religious leaders for peace.

There have been several recent world gatherings on international relations and peace involving religious personalities which must be catalogued at this time. Early in this decade Dr. Josef L. Hromadka of Prague, Czechoslovakia, convened the Christian Peace Conference; that conference has held two international meetings and will hold a third at the end of March. It has developed into a worldwide effort, not confined to the West, but so far it has been limited to Christians. Likewise, the Center for the Study of Democratic Institutions, located in California, convened two *Pacem in Terris* conferences, first in New York City in 1965, and then in Geneva in 1966. Some religious leaders attended both conferences, and the framework for both was the historic encyclical of Pope John XXIII; the auspices, however, were actually secular and not religious. A third postwar effort was the World Religionists' Conference for Peace convened in Kyoto in 1959 and in Tokyo in 1964. These received the participation of religious leaders especially from Japan, the Soviet Union, and China, but few from the West. All three of these international efforts —and no doubt there have been others—contributed to the necessary dialogue as religious leaders confront the hard problems of international relations and peace in the nuclear age.

The present United States inter-religious activity for peace was initiated early in this decade, by Rabbi Eisendrath, Dr. Greeley, Bishop John J. Wright, Bishop John Wesley Lord, Msgr. Edward G. Murray, and others. It resulted in the convening of almost 500 clergymen and laymen of the Judeo-Christian tradition as the National Inter-Religious Conference on Peace, held in Washington in March 1966. The final declaration of this conference asked the cochairmen—three of whom are participants at this New Delhi Symposium—to "explore the possibilities for calling a World Inter-Religious Conference on Peace in 1967, encompassing participation of all the world's religious traditions."

This resolution was not accepted lightly, but its implementation has been even more difficult than its sponsors envisioned. The U.S. Inter-Religious Committee on Peace—formed as a continuation of the National Conference held in Washington—sent the Rev. Herschel Halbert and me around the world in March and April 1967 to explore the possibilities of convening a world conference. We found, as our report shows, some readiness, many leaders, but no great initiative. We did discover, however, the willingness of the Gandhi Centenary Committee to cosponsor an initial, exploratory symposium as part of its series of seminars marking the birth of the great world leader. We are convened this week as part of this process. One of the several purposes of this Symposium, as you know, is to explore both the desirability and the feasibility of convening in the future a larger, broader world conference on religion and peace.

What would be the major purposes of convening a world conference on religion and peace? The first purpose would be to acquaint the leaders of world religions with the sanctions and traditions each major religion has within it for world peace and for more just international relations. This alone is a big order, as we are discovering from this Symposium. Just the exposure of religious leaders to each other, the acquaintanceship, is important in a shrinking world. Despite this shrinkage of space and thus time, and despite our growing mass-universal culture, we still know too little about each other's religions. Indeed, we may know more about our differing theologies than our common traditions in this important field of peace. To enhance and deepen this acquaintanceship would be one major purpose for a world conference on religion and peace.

A second purpose of a world conference would be to ascertain if, indeed, there are principles or middle axioms on international relations and peace which we do have in common—despite or because of our differing religious traditions and despite the strong infusion of our separate nationalisms in most of our religions today. Part of the work of a world conference would be to find common principles which would take priority over our differing national entanglements. Such a conference would emphasize that we are men and women of religion first, only Americans or Soviets or Indians or Japanese second. This is still a difficult exercise for many of us in a world of seemingly growing nationalisms. This effort to find common principles and axioms, based on religion, could well constitute a second purpose of a world conference.

Still another purpose of a world conference would be to discuss several specific international problems from the viewpoint of certain provisional common religious principles in the effort toward common action. What about the chronic problems, the crises of the common people? What about development, disarmament, and decolonialization which demand creative, permanent solutions? Some of our religious bodies have begun to evolve positions and even technical position papers on these and other major world issues. It is important that we begin to compare these positions and perhaps find common positions. Even if it is not possible to arrive at common solutions, a world conference could still discuss specific urgent problems, as we have just begun to do here.

The fourth purpose of a world conference would be to give heart to the people of the world, who are by and large religious people, that their religious leaders are working for peace which they so badly need and desire. The very news that such a world conference is being convened would be good news to the ears of the common people, good news if it did not raise their hopes too high. This is always a danger: that we cannot begin to achieve what we attempt. Yet surely our followers will not indict us for high aim. A fourth purpose of a world conference would be to show the world's people that world religions are indeed alive to the problems of peace in this world, as well as to the eternal problems of the spirit.

The final purpose of a world conference would be to develop a corps of coworkers across religious and national lines who might be called upon, indeed mobilized, in any international emergency. (One of the principal achievements of our earlier exploratory mission was to compile a list of kindred spirits in North Africa and Asia from half a dozen religious traditions. This compilation is in relatively active demand.) We have lived through international crises in the recent past: the Berlin crisis, the Cuban missile crisis, the West Asian war, and now Vietnam which is more chronic perhaps than an emergency. Through getting to know one another, it may be possible, perhaps under *ad hoc* auspices, to bring together selectively religious leaders who have earlier discovered one another at a world conference. Then they could take action for peace such as issuing joint statements or participating in joint deputations in specific crises, doing so irrespective of their particular religion or nationality, but from the perspective of their religions. This, too, could be one purpose of a world conference.

From this delineation of history and purpose, the desirabil-

ity of holding a world conference on religion and peace may
be increasingly clear to many. Certainly the vision is there.
Without vision the people perish; but without feasibility,
visions languish. How feasible is it to hold a world conference
in 1969 or 1970? What are some of the practical difficulties
if, in fact, the prior decision of desirability were made? The
practical problems include, of course, finances, but the problems are several and by no means are they limited to finances.

One of the greatest practical problems in holding a world
conference is to obtain the cooperation of world religious
leaders. Many of the official religious bodies tend to be con-
servative, slow-moving, and suspicious, even in what has been
called an ecumenical age. Thus even some religious bodies in
the West which herald ecumenism are often loath, in the
name of encouraging "a syncretistic attitude," to send official
representatives to any world conference on religion and peace.
Because of these and allied difficulties, we in the United States
so far have concluded that it is better to convene these initial,
pioneer conferences on an unofficial basis. This means inviting
key individuals, often the highest leaders, but as individuals
and not technically representing their organizations. In this
way obstacles can be overcome and we can move faster.

A second practical problem is that of not moving too fast.
Despite the great urgency of world peace, there is no point of
killing an effort soon after it is born. The convening of representatives of world religions is a task requiring great diplo-
matic skill, perhaps equal to, if not greater than, convening
representatives of world ideologies. Suspicions die slowly;
progress is slow. So the second obstacle in convening a world
conference is to overcome impatience by not taking large
steps too quickly.

A third practical problem in convening a world conference
is to secure an adequate staff. An international inter-religious
conference, as a domestic one involving representatives of
varying religions, requires senior, experienced staff. For this

Symposium, we have been fortunate in that the two sponsoring organizations, and their affiliates, have loaned senior staff. Our U.S. Inter-Religious Committee on Peace can draw upon the services of eight or ten qualified executives employed by religious bodies. My own denomination, for example, has given me two extended leaves of absence with pay, totaling as much as two months each, to help explore and then prepare for this Symposium. This is one small religious group's contribution to world peace and to the growing ecumenical movement; more selfishly, my denomination no doubt feels that my experiences will enhance my usefulness as its staff member. But all organizations, even religious organizations, are not so generous and farsighted. Few would be generous if the staff time extended to twelve or even eighteen months. Thus there is the possibility of needing to employ one or possibly two full-time staff members to prepare any more ambitious world conference. This requires not only considerable funds, but—more important—the availability of qualified, senior staff for relatively a short period of employment.

A fourth practical problem is the selection of the site for a world conference. We are all very grateful that the Gandhi Centenary Committee invited us here to India for this Symposium. In many ways this site has proved to be ideal and no problems of visas have arisen. And yet what country should be the venue for a larger world conference on religion and peace? If it is truly to be a world conference, invitations must be extended to religious leaders from all involved countries. Thus we must find a site where, for example, Buddhists from China and Jews from Israel will be just as welcome as Confucianists from Taiwan or Muslims from the United Arab Republic. By the time a world conference nears, no doubt other political tensions will be reflected religiously. If a site must be neutral politically, it is desirable that it also be neutral religiously, so that no one religious group will appear to dominate the conference. This factor may rule out holding a

conference in any of those great cities which are the head-
quarters for world religions, such as Rome, Geneva, Jerusalem, or Istanbul. But what politically and religiously neutral
cities remain? There has been a suggestion that Vienna might
be one ideal site. No doubt other suggestions will come, but
the problem is there.

A fifth practical problem is the quickly changing nature
of the political and of even the religious world. Our times are
marked, as perhaps never before, by cataclysmic changes.
What begins as a climate of peace turns overnight into an
environment of war. And yet if we decide now to convene
a larger world conference, we must be flexible to a point;
we cannot easily turn back. We have had our moments of
anxiety even with this Symposium, but the wars in West Asia,
including Cyprus, not to mention some of the internal
troubles in India, did not deter us. If, early in 1968, a world
conference to be held sometime in 1969 or 1970 looks desirable, then we must go ahead, whatever the political or religious climate in 1969 or 1970. We cannot allow rebellions,
revolutions, or war—or momentary peace—to deter us if we
decide to go ahead. That was the tragedy of the effort in the
nineteen thirties which we dare not repeat.

A world conference is toward the end of a long road.
The decision to walk that road should not be taken lightly.
On the other hand, the convening of a world conference appears inevitable. It is an idea whose time has come. If our
Symposium will not give such a world conference preliminary
if provisional endorsement, some other convention of religious
leaders is likely to do so soon. Yet the immediate decision is
now in your hands.

SYMPOSIUM CONCLUSIONS

1. A World Conference on Religion and Peace should be held, with the recommendation that a Permanent Council of the World's Religions for Peace with Justice should be developed following the Conference.

2. An Interim Advisory Committee should be formed.

3. The Joint Secretaries and Secretariat of the present Symposium should continue their work, with due attention being given to research and publication.

4. An attempt should be made to secure the collaboration of as many religious bodies as possible, in particular peace groups and movements within those religious bodies.

5. Each religion should look into its own tradition and to its sanctions for peace and reexamine, in the spirit of humility and courage, the reasons of its failure to be a more effective influence for peace.

6. The goal of a World Conference should be pressed with a sense of urgency as well as an awareness of the thoroughness necessary for the accomplishment of the task, remembering that great tasks cannot be accomplished too quickly.

7. All participants of this Symposium, moved by the dynamic of gratitude for the experience of high values gained, should use their influence within their own religious constituencies for the promotion of its objectives.

8. National and regional conferences should be held when possible as preliminary meetings to the World Conference and recognized as such when approved by the Interim Advisory Committee.

9. Finances and adequate resources for the World Conference should be sought from individuals, trusts, foundations, and religious bodies.

10. In view of the providential coincidence of the develop-

ment of a World Conference on Religion and Peace during the period of the Gandhi Centenary Celebration, the Conference should be held on or near Gandhi's birthday (October 2, 1969), if this proves feasible.

11. The choice of the venue of the World Conference should be made from the following list: New Delhi, The Hague, Rangoon, Vienna, Addis Ababa, Geneva, Colombo, Stockholm, or Nairobi.

Proposals

1. The Interim Advisory Committee shall be made up of the members of the present Steering Committee of the Symposium plus other members representing religious traditions not represented at the Symposium. This Interim Advisory Committee should contain a mixture of unofficial and official representatives of world religious groups. At an appropriate time, a representative Preparatory Committee should be appointed. This Interim Advisory Committee and/or representatives of absent members shall meet on January 16, 1968, in New Delhi in order to make initial plans for the Preparatory Committee and a World Conference.

2. The present Joint Secretaries and Secretariat shall continue with the following responsibilities: (*a*) Supervision of the publication of the proceedings of this Symposium. (*b*) Execution of the decisions made by the Interim Advisory Committee for the World Conference. The Secretariat shall be enlarged by paid and volunteer staff as directed.

3. The participants of this Symposium are charged with these responsibilities: (*a*) Interpreting the findings, recommendations, and spirit of this Symposium to the leaders and constituencies of their religions. (*b*) Enlisting the organizations and movements within their bodies devoted to the pursuit of world peace. (*c*) Exploring avenues for securing financial resources for the World Conference. (*d*) Promoting and organizing regional and national meetings.

9. ✍ CLOSING SESSION

THE TWELFTH AND CLOSING SESSION of the Symposium was again held in the auditorium of the International Center. Many guests had been invited in addition to participants and observers. Hon. Morarji Desai, Deputy Prime Minister of India, was chairman. A brief Christian service was led by Bishop Joseph L. Bernardin, Auxiliary Bishop of Atlanta, Georgia. Brief reports were given for the secretariat by Dr. Homer A. Jack, on the Symposium Message by Shri R. R. Diwakar, on the projected World Conference on Religion and Peace by Prof. K. G. Saiyadain, and on the three panels by Ven. Pimbure Soratha Thero, Bishop W. Q. Lash, and Dastoor N. D. Minochehr-Homji. Gov. Harold E. Stassen then gave an address, followed by the closing speech by Dr. Karan Singh.

Hon. Morarji Desai

IT IS GOVERNMENTS which have made wars, and not the people of any country. Being in government, I cannot easily claim to be a worker for peace. And yet my conscience is clear in this matter because I believe in peace and I am in government because my government believes in peace. If my government believed in the solution of problems by means of war, I would not be a part of the government. But that does not mean that we do not have to defend ourselves if we are attacked. If that were not our resolve, we would be putting a premium on violence, and there would not be even a remote faith in peace in any part of the world. Governments must, therefore, defend themselves. Mahatma Gandhi clarified this necessity.

It is only since World War II that people have begun to ask for peace. Earlier, most countries believed in war as a good instrument of progress. After the last war, the forces of destruction which resulted from the amazing advances that science has made have frightened people. Everybody is convinced now that, if there is a war, the mightiest also will have to suffer and will face destruction. There will be hardly any victor or any vanquished; both sides will be the vanquished.

It is fear which is making people believe in peace. As long as this belief is the outcome of fear, it will be difficult to devise all that is required in order to make peace a lasting actuality. Anything that is done out of fear can never lead to peace. Untruth and violence are resorted to only on account of fear. It is fear which is really the enemy of the good instincts of mankind. The bad instincts are encouraged by that fear. Since the preliminary step to peace has come out of a belief in peace, even if prompted by fear, more and more thinking about peace and more and more attempts at finding out how peace can be achieved will result in a growing conviction that peace is vital. Fear must be shed if peace is really to be achieved.

It is only the real spirit of religion which will enable man to be fearless and therefore to be human; man must become human in the real meaning of the term and also fearless. Otherwise, there is not much difference between man and the animals. It is only religion which elevates man from the level of the ordinary animal. But by religion I do not mean all that we profess and all that we deny in practice. By religion I mean the real spirit of religion. We say that we believe in religion, but most of us hardly act up to our beliefs. I do not say that all do not act in accordance with their beliefs. I am very happy that there are earnest seekers of the religious spirit and of peace who have gathered here at this Symposium. I cannot claim to be a man of religion as long as I have not acquired the fullest spirit of it. But I am certainly a humble seeker of the religious spirit and, therefore, I attach great importance to what has been done here at this Symposium.

If by religion we mean those who believe in God only, that would be a very narrow definition. It is not that those who do not believe in God have not the religious spirit. If they believe in truth, they are equally as religious as those who believe in God, because, in my view, there is no difference between truth and God. But those who believe in religion, that is in God, and still are not careful all the while, every moment of their lives, to tell the truth in every word that they utter, how can they claim that they are really following religion?

When we believe in God, we believe that God is present all the while everywhere. Then how can we deny him by telling lies? But that is what many people do and still they claim that they believe in religion. They believe in religion, but their faith is not that strong. Religion enables man to raise himself to the highest level. It is this which has to be brought about in the world by those who are real men of religion, a task they have been at from time immemorial, and it is a task which will continue. Otherwise there would be no hope for peace.

Why do I emphasize the highest aims in discussing religion? I do so because it is a fact of history that more violence and more bloodshed have been caused in the name of religion than anything else. Not in one country only but in all countries and by all religions. I do not think any religion can claim that it has been free from this wrong direction of its faith. It is therefore a very happy thing that men, believing in different religious faiths, come together, seek the common religious urge contained in all these religions, respect each other, and thereby translate their influence into the whole of society.

There are wars because there is greed, because there is a desire to own more than one can properly have without affecting the rights of somebody else. Unless the real spirit of religion is emphasized and lived, it will not be possible to bring peace to the world. I do believe that this is the goal which we shall reach one day. But even if we do not reach it, it is worth striving for all the while. If the attempt to bring peace to the world is not made, then violence will increase and the world will get worse and worse and not better and better.

It is the task for all of us to see that the world becomes better and better, so that peace is achieved at the end and the society of man becomes a real human society. Unless fear of each other disappears, and the disappearance of fear can happen only when one does not cast an evil eye on someone else's status in life; unless every country is determined not to make war on another on any account; unless every religion respects all religions and does not consider itself superior to others, there will be hardly any hope for transfusing the real religious spirit into the whole of human society. It is these things that I hope will be thought about more and more. At any rate, this is what I would urge. What creates all the disharmony which leads to war? It is because an individual wants something belonging to another individual which he takes by force making violence on him. But he does so only when the other party is weak. It is not the poor who make war. It is only the rich who make war because they want to have more and more riches. It is not the weak who make war, because they cannot do so. It is only the strong who want to make war because they want others to be subject to themselves. We must change this whole thing, which can only be accomplished by a real religious spirit. Unless the rich work for the poor and utilize their riches for the satisfaction of the poor and in that find satisfaction for themselves, it will be difficult to remove greed, hatred, and jealousy which are the real causes of war, either between individuals or countries. Only men of religion who constantly think about these things and who, by their lives exude that spirit and atmosphere in the society which envelops others, can strive for and achieve these aims.

We have to learn our own faults and infirmities. If we do not do so, and if we maintain a superior air, I am afraid that we will be the greatest impediments to peace. Unless ideas which in my view are fundamental are considered important enough, and unless we work to see that we create conditions by our own lives where strife is excluded from either discussion or in our transactions with each other we will not be able to create the necessary atmosphere for peace.

I was happy when I was told that there were no quarrels here at this Symposium and that everything went on peacefully. But there was nothing to be obtained by anybody from anybody here. Therefore there was peace. But if anybody had tried to force his views on somebody else, I do not know if there would have been this peace here. And strife is what is required to be excluded, and I am happy that it was excluded here. The next step would not be mere toleration, because toleration is a word of patronage, and patronization presupposes superiority and inferiority. It is a question of respect for the other person.

In Christianity it was said: "Do unto others as you want others to do unto you." But how many of us live like that? In Hinduism it is said: "I must act toward all living things as I expect those things to live with respect to me." From that came nonviolence. Only when one respects others can we have an atmosphere of equality. Somehow every religious community wants to expand itself. From this desire comes strife. It will have to be given up by religious communities if religion has to have its real functioning through the imperfect instruments which we are. It is this, I think, that requires more and more consideration, and it is a very hopeful sign that these are the things which are considered now more and more vital in the modern world.

Science has also advanced so much that it will enable us to see that nobody is in want. But science also is enabling us to forge instruments of destruction. Unless we change that and spiritualize science, science will not allow us to enjoy the benefit which it should really give to mankind. Peace, therefore, is vital, but vital peace has got to be earned by sacrifice and not by aggression.

Hon. Harold E. Stassen

WE TOGETHER HAVE HERE made a beginning. We have made a significant beginning toward combining the work for peace of major religions of the world. Do not underestimate the impact of what you together have here done. Because we met, the prospects of an early and honorable ending of the war in Vietnam and of the fair solution of the edge-of-war tensions in the Mideast are both a bit brighter. Because we met, the outlook for world peace is in a measure improved.

It has been long evident that the excellent separate work for peace of the various religious bodies of the world was inadequate and fell short of the mark. It has also been clear that the governmental leaders and diplomats and the present United Nations were not sufficiently effective for peace.

There has been and is an urgent need for the establishment of a definite worldwide moral climate, with reasonably precise outlines to nurture successful work for peace. This can only be established by the combined thoughtful and sustained endeavor of the major religions of the world. This we have here begun to do.

I would not now presume to speak for all of you, as there are, of course, some continuing differences of detailed views. But it has become evident that certain crucial comments may be made in reflection of virtual unanimity. When we speak of peace, we speak of peace with justice, or of peace and justice. We are convinced that the search for peace must have as an inseparable companion the search for justice. The definition of justice is not easy. Men will continue to ask through the ages, what is justice? We agree that it is unjust that any peoples who do their own best should be hungry, or lack shelter or clothing, or be deprived of educational opportunity, or be denied the fair and equal measure of stature and dignity before God and man. We agree that justice at best will be imperfect, even as peace at best will be troubled. But we emphasize that intelligent striving for peace with justice must be unceasing.

It follows that peace cannot be a product of the frozen status quo. There must be peaceful change, to correct injustices, to meet new conditions, to open new potentials for all peoples. Thus there is an imperative need for institutions of peaceful change and methods of peaceful solutions.

Here we ask the statesmen of the world to give consideration to modernizing and strengthening the United Nations so that new and improved structures for peace-making and peace-keeping will be established such as:

1. A United Nations board of arbitration,
2. A United Nations panel of mediators,
3. A world court for equitable peaceful solutions,

4. A dependable method of adequate financial support for peace-keeping institutions,

5. A small elite police force of young volunteers serving directly in a United Nations police force.

We ask continuing study and favorable consideration of the nonviolent methods of bringing about peaceful change from injustice, which have been successfully practiced by Mahatma Gandhi, Martin Luther King, Jr., and their associates. We recognize the different problems of defense against external violence and against violent aggression. Here we raise for study in this nuclear age the possible development of the principle of minimum violence; that is to say a response of minimum violence to defend against violence. We ask this study especially because the escalation of violence of response projects directly toward the holocaust of a nuclear war. Obviously a doctrine of minimum violence in a defensive response must not be permitted to encourage violent aggression. But the opinion of all mankind on the moral factors has a heavy weight in the final decisions of contests and attempts at aggression. Thorough studies are needed.

From our various religions we join in a universal concern for all humanity on this earth under God. Thus we urge that this universal principle be reflected in the representation of all peoples within the United Nations, even though this may require two member governments, for those people who are now divided by reason of the aftermath of World War II and of the divisions in the world: the Germans, Chinese, Vietnamese, and Koreans.

We respectfully ask the leaders of all religions in the world to consider participating in a future world conference of religions for peace and justice. I would anticipate 1970 as a logical year. I would suggest Colombo, Stockholm, or The Hague as potential locations. I would expect two or three thousand delegates to be an appropriate number. I would hope that a continuing world council of religions for peace and justice would emerge from such a conference with a definite charter, and with the potential of formulating moral pronouncements and of providing moral guidance for the conduct of nation states and of the United Nations.

May I state directly that in joining in this inter-religious movement for peace and justice I consider that I am being faithful to my own religious convictions, even as I take it you each do so consider for yourselves. Explicitly, I am a man with a deep and abiding lifelong faith in God and a firm belief in Jesus Christ. My religious convictions impel me to reach out to work with you for peace and justice, and to so work with humility and with perseverance. There is a passage in our Christian scriptures which reads: "Inasmuch as ye have done it unto one of these, even the least of them, ye have done it unto me." I know full well that, if man inflicts modern nuclear war upon humanity, what will thereby be done unto all of the peoples of the earth will be tragic beyond description.

The world is now a village. All of the people now live on Main Street. We must together build for peace and justice. I do believe we can succeed. For I do hold that man by his inherent nature as a child of God was meant to be free and meant to be at peace!

Karan Singh

IT IS INDEED FITTING that India has been chosen as the venue of this Symposium because our watchword from the dawn of our civilization is well summed up in the Rigvedic dictum: "Let noble thoughts come to us from every side."

India has for many centuries been the home and the haven for almost every religion which we find in the world today.

In the history not only of India but of the entire human race, religion has played a tremendously powerful and important role in the growth of the human being and his evolution from his animal nature into the human state in which we find ourselves today. This growth can continue into supermanhood. The evolution of man from his cave ancestry through the tribe, clan, and state has, through religion, given the impetus for some of the greatest and noblest creations of mankind in art, architecture, literature, and every sphere of human activity. Man has never really ever lived by bread alone. There has always been this other dimension of the human quest. Religion therefore has been responsible for a many-splendored achievement by the human race.

At the same time, I think it must be admitted that there has been a less-glowing side to the history of religion. Religion has also been responsible for unspeakable horrors, or at least horrors that have been perpetrated in the name of religion. People have been thrown to the lions, people have been burned at the stake, and all sorts of terrible things have been done in the name of religion. There has been conflict, massacre, and annihilation. Therefore, the history of religion and its performance today are checkered, by shadow and sunlight, by darkness and brightness.

As in the past the question that faces us today is what of the future? Mankind today finds itself at a crossroad. On the one hand, science and technology have given man the power to bring about unprecedented progress and prosperity. It has become possible now for us, if we use our power wisely, to banish disease, poverty, and ignorance from the face of this earth and perhaps even to wipe every tear from every eye. On the other hand, this same power, if it is wrongly used, can lead not only to the annihilation of the human race but of all life on this planet. Therefore the question really is whether religion, as a modern contemporary force, is going to be able to help in this process of choice. Is it going to become increasingly irrelevant, increasingly obsolete, and increasingly peripheral to the mainstream of human endeavor? Or is religion going to bring about a new awakening, a new upsurge, a new hope? Mankind today, with all its economic progress, is still groping for a new integration, is still groping for a new light. Among the younger generation in the world today, this groping is all the more desperate because the old is dying and the new is yet to be born. We find ourselves in a period of transition, in which we look for new light. Can religion fill this vacuum? My own personal feeling is that religion can do so indeed, but there are three prerequisites.

Religion has got to accept openheartedly and fully science and all its implications. This does not mean that we must accept all the applications of science. But the findings and facts of science have got to be accepted, integrated, and made part of our conscience. Science today is probing into the vastness of outer space. We are going into galaxies billions of light years away through new mechanisms and through new science and we are going into the very structure of the human cell. This probing, this magnificent achievement of science—which is a tremendous monument to man's industry and intelligence—is with us and we must bridge this dichotomy between science and religion. It must not be necessary for modern man to choose between science and religion. If you pose this choice to him, it will be a traumatic choice; and it will militate against that integration which is the real purpose of religion. Therefore, the first prerequisite is that science has got to be accepted wholeheartedly.

Inter-religious tolerance is no longer sufficient; genuine understanding is essential. At one time, tolerance used to be looked upon as a very great virtue. But tolerance is negative. We need more than tolerance. We need an active and sympathetic understanding between the different religions of the world. It is only then that that degree of empathy will be generated which will enable religions to work together. It would be most helpful if, instead of stressing dogma and ritual, we stress that essential unity that exists in every religion. There have been different paths, as the Upanishad says. In the same way that many streams arising from different places ultimately find their way into the same ocean, in the same way that to one mountain peak there are different paths and different routes, similarly, we must accept the fact that different religions go to the same goal. Here it is that the voice of the mystic can help us because, in every religion, in every climate, in every country, and in every age, there have arisen men and women who have shown us this path. They have spoken in the language of myth and symbol. They have said that the divine voice is there resounding around us with the crash of a thousand seas if we only have the ears to hear. The vision is there exploding in front of our eyes with the majesty of a thousand suns if we only have the eyes to see. It is with those ears and those eyes that we must look upon religion today and acknowledge the integrating force between the different religions.

The concept of the dignity of God is no longer adequate for us. We have got to move on to the concept of the dignity of man. The Upanishad has a word for mankind: "children of immortality." Every human being who comes into this world is born with a divine spark. This has got to be given the full opportunity to grow into the mighty flame of realization. Unless this is accepted and unless we are quite clear in our minds about this, I do not really see how religion can become a force for world peace. It is only the concept of the dignity of man that will give us that golden thread which binds every member of the human race to the other. This thread binds both those who believe in religion and those who do not necessarily believe in religion. It is a concept which has got to be accepted.

If these three concepts are accepted by modern religion—the importance of science, the importance of a genuine understanding and empathy between different religions, and the concept of the dignity of man—it is only then that religion really will be able to become a force for world peace.

The world today awaits a new light. It is for those who are dedicated to religion to give that light. Then in a world torn by hatred, suspicion, fear, and jealousy, a new integration will be born. All the greatness that religion has done will grow into this final achievement. All the sins that have been perpetrated in the name of religion will be washed away if we are able at this crucial juncture to give the correct lead to mankind.

1. Rev. G. Nichidatsu Fujii[1]

BY DELIVERANCE (*vimoksha*) is meant the joy of being liberated from all sorts of sufferings, afflictions, and illnesses. According to Buddhism, life in this world is full of sufferings and worries. Although these sufferings and distresses are numberless in kind, they are roughly divided into the four main sufferings of life, old age, illness, and death. The result of spiritual searchings and physical endeavors for the purpose of being liberated from the sufferings of life, old age, illness, and death is the raised standard of social life called civilization.

The present civilization has succeeded in easing somewhat the difficulties of life, the first of the four great sufferings, and also in alleviating the sufferings of illness, and in lengthening the average life of human beings. But the sufferings of death have hurled the human race into the bottom of sufferings, together with unnatural sufferings and fears. Mankind has never been exposed so helplessly as it is today to the suffering of the most miserable and large-scale death due to the violence of what is called war.

[1] This paper was circulated to the Symposium but not delivered orally.

A frog is swallowed by a snake, a rat eaten by a cat, and a pheasant by an eagle. This state of affairs has been feared as the sufferings of the beastly world. Further, there are the 136 sufferings of hell which have been feared by mankind since ancient times as the most horrible sufferings. However, it is the modern war in which highly refined scientific weapons of mass extermination are employed that may bring sufferings and damage thousands of times greater than the sufferings of the hells, and may spell the miserable death and total destruction of mankind.

However loudly the warmongers may shout about freedom and peace, and however many treaties they may conclude, they cannot justify the indiscriminate massacre and destruction that they are committing ceaselessly day and night. Modern war is more barbarous than the world of beasts and poisonous reptiles and the prison guards of hell. It is a curse and at the same time a lesson to humanity.

The most formidable enemy that threatens the human race with total extinction is not different ideologies, different religions, or different nations, but the armament race in which contemporary states and military alliances are engaged.

There is only one way for mankind to be delivered from its total destruction. Mahatma Gandhi called it nonviolence and achieved a bloodless revolution in India, leading the independence movement of that country.

In ancient times, wise men left their castles and mansions, wives and children, abandoned arms and weapons, riches and possessions, and practiced nonviolence in mountains and forests. Their deeds and words benefited the ordinary people. This was unavoidable in times when traffic and means of communications were not so advanced as they are today.

Nonviolence should start from the home. It can be practiced by anyone. If this is practiced in the home, homes will be filled with love and mercy so that no one will do violence to any other member of the home even if he or she commits an error.

At a time when means of communication and transportation have developed to such an extent where the entire world seems to have become very small, it is very reasonable to regard the world as one family. Mahatma Gandhi, believing in nonviolence, developed the greatest movement of collective nonviolence in the world and finally successfully carried out a political revolution through the means of nonviolence which achieved independence and freedom for India. As Mahatma Gandhi himself said, this was the greatest achievement that a single nation had made to contribute toward the safeguarding of world peace. He once said:

> I must express my belief that an independent India had better reject all violence even for defending its national borders. It would be suicidal for India to join in the armament race. If India should lose nonviolence, the world would lose its last hope. . . . I have the firm conviction that it is the mission of India to spread the gospel of nonviolence throughout the world. It may take long years for it to be developed. But, according to my judgment, no other nation would outstrip India in the fulfillment of this mission. It is extremely timely for India to promote the significance of this mission. . . .

Soon after independence, India resorted to military action in frontier disputes. It is also creating a modern army. India will have to follow a slow and tortuous course before she finally attains the great goal of nonviolence, just as an infant falters and falls before it can walk straight.

After World War II, Japan was the first nation to proclaim in its new constitution abandonment of all military potential and the renunciation of the right to go to war. However, after the Korean War, Japan was forced, under pressure, to increase her military might in the name of national self-defense, until today she has an armament more powerful than she had in the past days of militarism.

Following the principle of "might is right," and of the survival of the fittest, which should be reserved to beastly life, modern states are pursuing the course of military aggrandisement, praising the art of killing, and thus discarding world peace as a dream of the foolish.

World peace cannot be attained until the world's powers have totally abolished their military potentials. The armament race among the world powers will ultimately lead mankind to a war of total extermination. But mankind cannot be so foolish as to permit itself to be destroyed totally.

Can't the way be found for mankind's deliverance in time before its total destruction? It can be found only through the spiritual might of nonviolence as opposed to physical and mechanical violence. Victory and supremacy based on murder and destruction by weapons will crumble easily. Spiritual supremacy founded on nonviolence will reign forever together with truth and law.

Since all the powers of the world consider violence and military armament to be the only guarantee for security, it appears that they cannot be brought easily to agree to the total abolition of armaments.

However, we see in Indian independence the real superiority of nonviolence to violence and to arms and their effectiveness. No one can deny this fact. It is essential for the idea of nonviolence to grip the minds of the people of the world and for the people of the world to launch a coordinated collective movement to cool the high fever of the disease that "might is right," and that "violence settles everything." It is through this way that powerful nations can be brought to agree to total abolition of armaments and that world peace can be realized.

Namu myoho renge kyo! Glory to the sutra of the lotus of the supreme law!

2. The Japanese-American Inter-Religious Consultation on Peace

THE JAPANESE-AMERICAN INTER-RELIGIOUS CONSULTATION ON PEACE was held in Kyoto on January 22, 1968. Inspired by the U.S. Inter-Religious Committee on Peace, this Consultation was organized by an *ad hoc* Japanese committee headed by the Rev. Riri Nakayama, chief priest of the Buddhist temple Hozenji in Tokyo, and Dr. Shinichiro Imaoka, president of the Japan Free Religious Fellowship. The purpose of the Consultation was to take advantage of the presence in Japan of twelve persons from the U.S. Committee returning from attendance at the International Inter-Religious Symposium on Peace in New Delhi. The members of the Japanese committee wanted to confer with their American counterparts as well as to explore the possibility of a larger world conference on religion and peace.

The Japanese Consultation began with a formal dinner at the Okazaki Hotel in Kyoto. This was largely ceremonial, with some forty Japanese religious and educational leaders meeting for the first time with their American colleagues. Dr. Imaoka recalled the first Japanese Conference for International Peace Through Religion of May 1931. This was also held on American initiative and he had also been active in its preparation—thirty-seven years earlier! A proposed world conference, scheduled for Washington in 1932, was repeatedly postponed and the outbreak of World War II canceled it altogether. Dr. Imaoka was glad that Americans were once again taking leadership. World War III must not be allowed to break out. A world conference on religion and peace would be a culmination of man's dreams after 300,000 years of human existence on earth. He revealed his hope that, although he is close to ninety years of age, he would not die before his dream of peace was fulfilled. He is continuously rejuvenated by his undying faith that the world will find its way to peace. Indeed, the very fact that United States and Japanese religious leaders were meeting in an area of the world ravaged by war between these same two peoples was an omen of hope showing how erstwhile enemies can work together for peace. Then Rev. Kosho Otani, heir apparent to the abbacy of the Higashi Honganji, a Buddhist temple in Kyoto, gave a toast for "world peace and for the health of all of us here."

Mr. Yasheta, representing the Japanese committee, said that Kyoto was selected as the site for the Consultation because old religious traditions still prevail. While Japanese and American religious traditions do differ, world peace can be explored in such an atmosphere. Dr. Dana McLean Greeley, representing the U.S. Committee, declared that the Consultation was a "happy final chapter" for the world tour of the U.S. Committee. He thanked especially the Rev. Nakayama and Dr. Imaoka for initiating the Consultation. Rabbi Maurice N. Eisendrath gave a toast for peace, adding, "He who saves a single soul saves the entire world." Toshihiro Kennoki, former federal minister of education, gave an address of welcome, concluding also with a toast. Finally Rev. Koun Shigaragi pointed out that the Imperial Palace in Kyoto has no boundary of wall or water—and that lack of barrier should be reflected in the Consultation which should be conducted in this same unwalled spirit.

The principal meetings of the Consultation were held in the new International Conference Hall outside Kyoto. One of the smaller meeting rooms, equipped with simultaneous translating equipment, was used for the morning and afternoon sessions. At noontime, after lunch, the participants adjourned to the garden where in an appropriate teahouse, flower-arranging and tea pouring ceremonies were held.

The Japanese attendance at this Consultation spanned a wide range of religious leadership. The Buddhists were represented by Abbot Kosho Otani, Rev. Riri Nakayama and a ninety-year-old abbot, Daiko Furukema. In addition there were two members of the Nichiren sect: Rev. Gyojun Imai and Rev. Hidemitsu Usunomiya. The former is secretary-general of the Nichi-Indo Sarvodaya Friendship Association. Also present was Rev. Gyomei Kubose, pastor of the Buddhist church in Chicago, president of the American Buddhist Association, and a temporary resident of Kyoto. Representing the new religions arising from Buddhism was Rev. Nikkyo Niwano, head of Rissho Kosei Kai and Rev. Kinzo Takemura. Also present was Shuten Oishi, managing director of the Union of the New Religious Organizations of Japan.

The Shintoists were also well represented. Yoshitaka Takahara, chief priest of the Yasaka shrine, was a participant as were representatives from sectarian Shintoism: Rev. Toshio Miyako of Konkokyo and Kyosho Mizutani from Tenrikyo.

Both Protestants and Roman Catholics participated. Rev. Joseph J. Spae, director of the Oriens Institute of Religious Research, was present as was Rev. Yojiro Tomon. Protestants included Kenneth E. Jones of the Kyodan (the United Church of Japan) and Rev. Tetsutaro Ariga, formerly director of the Center for the Study of Japanese Religions in Kyoto.

Among the miscellaneous groups represented, in addition to Dr. Imaoka of the Japan Free Religious Association, were two delegates of Oomoto: Rev. Isao Deguchi and Kiyohido Mori.

Cochairmen for the Consultation were Yasuyoshi Sakata of the Japan Religious League and Dr. Greeley. During the preliminaries, the ninety-year-old abbot, Daiko Furukema, urged that the Consultation find a way to peace quickly. He declared that, when we respect others, we also respect ourselves. He asked that we rid ourselves of unnecessary desires, including the desires of all people for their own selfish ends. In ridding oneself of selfishness, one rids oneself of isolation. The suffering of one, he insisted, must be the suffering of all.

When we feel this way we will find a way to alleviate suffering and this will lead to peace. Later he made a presentation to each of the participants of a calligraphic symbolization of peace.

Bishop John Wesley Lord briefed participants on the New Delhi Symposium. Rev. Kosho Otani spoke about Buddhism with special reference to peace, Rev. Yoshitaka Takahara spoke about Shintoism also with reference to peace, and Bishop John H. Burt discussed the Judeo-Christian tradition of peace. After luncheon, the Consultation discussed a possible world conference on religion and peace and what practical contributions inter-religious groups in Japan and the United States could make for the realization of world peace. After some debate, a committee was appointed to draw up a report for submission to the final session.

The debate on the current world situation sparked discussion of Vietnam. Dr. Greeley stated that "many of us Americans believe that the United States government is on the wrong track." Bishop Burt said that, since neither party is willing to take the initiative in going to the negotiation table, "our best hope for a solution is a third force." He asked Japanese religious leaders to urge their government to take a more active role, either alone or in concert with other Asian countries in peace-making efforts "in the name of humanity." Rabbi Eisendrath discussed the relation between Pearl Harbor and Hiroshima and the guilts arising therefrom.

At the meeting of the drafting committee, there was considerable hesitation on the Japanese side about formulating the joint communiqué. In discussing a possible world conference, the Interim Advisory Committee growing out of the New Delhi Symposium suggested that it be held in 1969 as part of the centenary of the birth of Gandhi. Some Japanese delegates were successful in omitting this reference.

The final communiqué, as adopted by the Committee and then by the whole Consultation, reads as follows:

1. The participants in the Japanese-American Inter-Religious Consultation on Peace, meeting in Kyoto on January 22, 1968, heard a report on the International Inter-Religious Symposium on Peace that was held in New Delhi earlier this month from a delegate of the United States who attended that Symposium. This presentation was followed by a useful discussion on the report. Delegates from Japan expressed their full agreement with the spirit of the New Delhi Conference.

2. We recognize that it is opportune to hold a world religious conference for peace in the second half of 1969 or the first half of 1970.

3. The participants in this Consultation recognize that it is meaningful to provide opportunities to talk about peace among leaders of the various religions in Asia.

4. We also believe that further efforts should be made for international inter-religious cooperation for peace in an appropriate form, including a possible second Japanese-American Inter-Religious Conference.

The Japanese participants held several meetings subsequent to the Consultation in Kyoto. The purpose of one was to explore the possibility of a regional meeting to help end the war in Vietnam. Another was held to explore the establishment of a Japanese Inter-Religious Committee on Peace. In April the informal committee decided to entrust the task for convening a national consultation in Japan to the existing Japan Inter-Religious Federation.

3. The Interim Advisory Committee for a World Conference on Religion and Peace

THE INTERNATIONAL INTER-RELIGIOUS SYMPOSIUM ON PEACE voted at its final plenary session that "a World Conference on Religion and Peace should be held" and "an Interim Advisory Committee should be formed." The plenary also recommended that "the Interim Advisory Committee shall be made up of members of the present Steering Committee of the Symposium plus other members representing religious traditions not represented at the Symposium."

To take advantage of the presence in New Delhi of some of these persons, the first meeting of the Interim Advisory Committee was held in New Delhi on January 16, 1968. Archbishop Angelo Fernandes was asked to take the chair for the meeting. In addition to Archbishop Fernandes, those present included Msgr. Edward G. Murray, Dr. Gopal Singh, Dastoor N. D. Minochehr-Homji, Bishop James K. Mathews, Prof. M. Yamunacharya, Rabbi André Zaoui, Shri G. Ramachandran, Dr. Homer A. Jack, Rabbi Maurice N. Eisendrath, Dr. Dana McLean Greeley, Herman Will, Jr., Patrick deSouza, Gov. Harold E. Stassen, Shri R. Achuthan, and Shri Krishna Kumar.

After an evaluation of the Symposium, and the making of arrangements for the publication of its proceedings (in part in *Gandhi Marg* and fully in a volume to be produced in the United States), plans were made for the composition and work of the Interim Advisory Committee.

Six members present who were members of the steering committee of the Symposium agreed to serve; the exception was Archbishop Fernandes, who wanted more time to consider the invitation. Thus those initially accepting included Monsignor Murray, Dr. Singh, Dastoor Minochehr-Homji, Bishop Mathews, Professor Yamunacharya, and Rabbi Zaoui. Those members of the steering committee who could not be present, but sent regrets, included Jamel D. Gomboev, Rev. Riri Nakayama, and Prof. K. G. Saiyadain. It was voted to ask the following persons also to serve: Shri R. R. Diwakar and Ven. Pimbure Soratha Thero. Additional members invited will include representatives from Shintoism, the Greek

Orthodox church, the Vatican Secretariat on Justice and
Peace, and religionists from Africa and Latin America. It
was also agreed that a presidium of between five and nine
persons should be named, with the two joint secretaries fully
selecting this representative group of leaders without any hur-
ried attempts to crystallize its membership. The proposal of
the Symposium that the two joint secretaries of the Symposium—Shri G. Ramachandran, M.P., and Dr. Homer A.
Jack—continue as joint secretaries of the Interim Committee
was confirmed, with the addition of other staff from the
Symposium secretariat as needed. A small, international group
of honorary sponsors for the World Conference will also be
named.

It was tentatively agreed to convene the World Conference
during the last days of December 1969, and early 1970, in
order to coincide with the Gandhi Centenary Year (1969),
and the twenty-fifth anniversary of the establishment of the
United Nations (1970), of the end of World War II (1970),
and of the beginning of the development decade (1970).
Additional explorations must be made on determining the
venue of the conference. It was also agreed to stimulate the
holding of national and regional conferences, perhaps with
the help of a syllabus to be prepared. These conferences
would help channel intent and personnel to the World Conference. It was further decided that the secretariat should
begin to stimulate the canvassing of official world religious
bodies to ascertain their interest in the World Conference. An
initial approach would be for such bodies to appoint an individual or subcommittee to study the Symposium proceedings and plans for the World Conference and then to make a
recommendation for official or unofficial participation.

The proposal was accepted that the Interim Advisory Committee would cease early in 1969, holding only one meeting.
This Interim Advisory Committee would be succeeded by a
preparatory committee which would meet early in 1969 and

continue in operation until the beginning of the World Conference.

A finance subcommittee was appointed to make plans for supporting the work of the Interim Advisory Committee. Consisting of Dr. Singh, Gov. Stassen, and Rabbi Zaoui, this subcommittee also met on January 16. A budget through 1968 was projected of 195,000 rupees ($26,000). This would cover secretariat expenses, secretariat travel, transportation for twenty members of the Interim Committee to one meeting, and contingencies. Quotas were assigned to religious leaders in several countries to raise this budget during 1968. It was also agreed to solicit some funds from founding sponsors or contributors, persons who would contribute above a stated amount (which might differ in each nation) and who would be recorded at the World Conference as founding contributors. Attempts will be made to raise funds from other sources, including religious bodies and foundations, although securing the substantially larger budget was to be the task of the preparatory committee.

Since January 16, 1968, efforts have begun to implement these decisions. A group of honorary sponsors is being organized as is the presidium and the membership of the total committee. The committee hopes to hold its first full meeting early in 1969.

4. Symposium Participants

Dr. Ralph D. Abernathy, Vice-President-Treasurer, Southern Christian Leadership Conference, 334 Auburn Avenue, N.E., Atlanta, Georgia 30303, U.S.A. Christian (Progressive National and American Baptist). (Also Mrs. Abernathy.) [He has since become President of SCLC.]

Shalome Abraham, Retired Principal, Sir Jacob Sassoon High School, 30/32 Parel, Bombay 12, India. Jewish.

Le Roy Anderson, Conrad, Montana, U.S.A. Christian (United Presbyterian).

Mrs. Aryanayakam Asha Devi, Sevagram, Wardha, Maharashtra, India. Hindu.

Ven. L. Ariyawansa, Mahabodi Society, Birla Temple, New Delhi, India. Buddhist.

Most Rev. Joseph L. Bernardin, V.G., Auxiliary Bishop of Atlanta, 136 W. Wesley Road, N.W., Atlanta, Georgia 30305, U.S.A. Christian (Roman Catholic).

Ven. Swami Bhaskaranandji, Suraj Kot Hill, New Delhi 14, India. Hindu. (Also B. L. Kapur, Secretary to the Swami.)

Dr. Desmond W. Bittinger, Chancellor, Chapman College, 904 E. Everett Place, Orange, California 92667, U.S.A. Christian (Church of the Brethren).

Dr. Bool Chand, Director, Ahiṁsā Shodh-Peeth, Ahiṁsā Bhavan, Shankar Road, Delhi 5, India. Jain.

Rt. Rev. John H. Burt, Bishop Coadjutor of Ohio, 2230 Euclid Avenue, Cleveland, Ohio 44115, U.S.A. Christian (Episcopal).

Shri R. R. Diwakar, M.P., Chairman, Gandhi Peace Foundation, 223 Rouse Avenue, New Delhi, India. Hindu.

Rabbi Maurice N. Eisendrath, President, Union of American Hebrew Congregations, 838 Fifth Avenue, New York, New York 10021, U.S.A. Jewish, Cochairman, U.S. Inter-Religious Committee on Peace. (Also Mrs. Eisendrath.)

Archbishop Angelo Fernandes, Archbishop of Delhi, Secretary, Catholic Bishops' Conference of India, C.B.C.I. Centre, Alexandra Place, New Delhi 1, India. Christian (Roman Catholic).

Most Rev. G. Nichidatsu Fujii, President, Nichi-Indo Sarvodaya Friendship Association, 2-23, 3-chome, Kita, Kudan,

Chiyodoku, Tokyo, Japan. Buddhist. (Also Miss Katsuko Horiuchi, Interpreter.)

Dr. Dana McLean Greeley, President, Unitarian Universalist Association (of the United States and Canada), 25 Beacon Street, Boston, Massachusetts 02108, U.S.A. Unitarian Universalist. Cochairman, U.S. Inter-Religious Committee on Peace.

Jambel D. Gomboev, Bandido Hambo Lama, Chairman, Religious Board of the Buddhists of the U.S.S.R., Ivolginsky Buddhist Temple, Ulan-Ude, U.S.S.R. Buddhist. (Also Miss Galya Tsybanova, Interpreter.)

Shri D. K. Gupta, Secretary, Gandhi Memorial Trust, Rajghat, New Delhi 1, India. Hindu.

Rev. Herschel Halbert, Secretary for International Affairs, The Episcopal Church, 815 Second Avenue, New York, New York 10017, U.S.A. Christian (Episcopal). Secretariat, U.S. Inter-Religious Committee on Peace.

Dr. Dorothy Hutchinson, Friends Coordinating Committee on Peace, 904 Rydal Road, Jenkintown, Pennsylvania 19046, U.S.A. Christian (Quaker).

Dr. Homer A. Jack, Director, Division of Social Responsibility, Unitarian Universalist Association, 25 Beacon Street, Boston, Massachusetts 02108, U.S.A. Unitarian Universalist. Secretariat, U.S. Inter-Religious Committee on Peace. (Also Mrs. Jack.)

Jagadguru Shri Gangadhar Rajayogeendra Mahaswamiji, Moorusavirmath, Hubli, India. Hindu.

Rt. Rev. W. Q. Lash, St. Clement, Truro, Cornwall, England. Christian (Anglican).

Bishop John Wesley Lord, Bishop, The Methodist Church, Washington Area, 100 Maryland Avenue, N.E., Washington, D.C. 20002, U.S.A. Christian (Methodist). Cochairman, U.S. Inter-Religious Committee on Peace. (Also Mrs. Lord.)

Bishop James K. Mathews, Bishop, The Methodist Church,

Boston Area, 581 Boylston Street, Boston, Massachusetts 02116, U.S.A. Christian (Methodist). (Also Mrs. Mathews and Miss Mathews.)

Dastoor N. D. Minochehr-Homji, Petit Fasali, Atash-Kadeh, 44 New Marine Lines, Fort, Bombay 1, India. Zoroastrian.

Rev. Telford Mook, Board of World Missions (Southeast Asia), 475 Riverside Drive, New York, New York 10027, U.S.A. Christian (United Church of Christ and Disciples of Christ).

Prof. M. Mujeeb, Vice Chancellor, Jamia Millia Islamia, Jamianagar, New Delhi, India. Muslim.

Msgr. Edward G. Murray, Sacred Heart Rectory, 169 Cummins Highway, Roslindale, Massachusetts 02131, U.S.A. Christian (Roman Catholic). Secretary-Treasurer, U.S. Inter-Religious Committee on Peace.

Rev. Riri Nakayama, Chairman, Buddha Worshippers' Association in Japan, Hozenji, 24-2 3-chome, Akabane-Dat, Kitaku, Tokyo, Japan. Buddhist.

Peer Zamin Nizami, Syed Bokhari, Head Priest, Sajjada-hanshin, Dargah Hazrat Khwaja Nizamuddin Aulia Dargahi Market, New Delhi, India. Muslim.

Rt. Rev. Bishop Phillip B. Parmar, Bishop of Delhi, 1 Church Lane, New Delhi, India. Christian (Anglican).

Princess Poon Pismai Diskul, President, World Fellowship of Buddhists, 41 Phra Athit Street, Bangkok, Thailand. Buddhist.

Shri G. Ramachandran, M.P., Secretary, Gandhi Peace Foundation, 223 Rouse Avenue, New Delhi 1, India. Sarvodaya Universalist.

Swami Ranganathananda, The Ramakrishna Mission Institute of Culture, Gol Park, Calcutta 29, India. Hindu.

Prof. K. G. Saiyadain, Asian Institute of Educational Planning and Administration, Indraprastha Estate, New Delhi, India. Muslim.

Aiem Sangkhavasi, Hon. General Secretary, World Fellowship of Buddhists, 41 Phra Athit Street, Bangkok, Thailand. Buddhist.

Dr. Gopal Singh, M.P., 62 South Avenue, New Delhi, India. Sikh.

Bishop Mangal Singh, Methodist Bishop of Delhi, 12 Boulevard Road, Delhi 6, India. Christian (Methodist).

Dr. Jay Holmes Smith, Chairman, Purana Swaraj Movement, Shri Aurbindo Ashram, New Delhi 16, India. Universal.

Ven. Pimbure Soratha Thero, Secretary-General, World Buddhist Sangha Council, Pirivena Road, Mt. Lavinia, Colombo 1, Ceylon. Buddhist.

Hon. Harold E. Stassen, Stassen and Kephart, 1020 Fidelity Building, 123 South Broad Street, Philadelphia, Pennsylvania 19109, U.S.A. Christian (American Baptist).

S. Vasudevan, 32 Jalan Angsana Setapar, Kuala Lumpar, Malaysia. Bahai.

Herman Will, Jr., Associate General Secretary, Methodist Division of Peace and World Order, 100 Maryland Avenue, N.E., Washington, D.C. 20002, U.S.A. Christian (Methodist). Secretariat, U.S. Inter-Religious Committee on Peace.

Ven. Baddeeama Wimalawansa Thero, Principal, Shri Lanka Vidyalaya, Colombo, Ceylon. Buddhist.

Prof. M. Yamunacharya, Gandhi Peace Foundation, 223 Rouse Avenue, New Delhi 1, India. Hindu.

Rabbi André Zaoui, Union Liberale Israelite, 24 Rue Copernic, Paris 16, France. Jewish.

Observers

Prof. Pouro Baldenjapov, Senior Adviser, Central Religious Board of the Buddhists of the U.S.S.R., 5/16 Mubina Street, Ulanude, U.S.S.R. Buddhist.

Miss Margaret Barr, Kharang, P.O. Shillong 7, Assam, India. Unitarian.

Ven. V. Dharmawara, Ashoka Mission, P.O. Mehrauli, New Delhi, India. Buddhist.

Bato Dougarov, V. V. Torei, District Djidinsky, U.S.S.R. Buddhist.

Selig Goodman, Quaker International Centre, 224 Jorbagh, New Delhi 3, India. Christian (Quaker).

Karnail Singh, Secretary, Gurunanak Foundation, 3 Jorbagh, New Delhi, India. Sikh.

Dr. Harold Snyder, Quaker International Affairs Representative for South Asia, 224 Jorbagh, New Delhi 3, India. Christian (Quaker).

Dr. R. N. Varma, Director, School of Law, University of Rajasthan, Jaipur, India. Hindu.

Speakers and Additional Leaders

Dr. Zakir Husain, President of India, Rashtrapati Bhavan, New Delhi, India. Muslim.

Sheikh Abdullah, 3 Ferozshah Road, New Delhi, India. Muslim.

Prof. Nirmal Kumar Bose, Commissioner, Scheduled Castes and Tribes, West Block No. 1, Wing No. 7, R. K. Puram, New Delhi 22, India.

Hon. Morarji Desai, Deputy Prime Minister of India, New Delhi 1, India. Hindu.

Rev. A. J. Fonscca, S.J., Editor, *Social Action*, Indian Social Institute, South Extension II, D-25-D, New Delhi 16, India. Christian (Roman Catholic).

Shri Jayaprakash Narayan, Kadomkuan, Patna 3, India.

Shri Pyare Lal Nayar, Flat 25, Shankar Market, Connaught Place, New Delhi 1, India. Hindu.

Dr. Karan Singh, Minister of Transport, Government of India, New Delhi, India. Hindu.

Staff

Shri G. Ramachandran, M.P., Joint Secretary
Dr. Homer A. Jack, Joint Secretary
Shri R. Achuthan, Assistant Secretary*
Rev. Herschel Halbert, Assistant Secretary
Shri Krishna Kumar, Chief of Press and Publicity*
Shri Vishnu Dutt, Press**
Theodore Schiller, Press****
Henry Hampton, Press*****
T. K. Mahadevan, Radio and Proceeding*
Prof. M. Yamunacharya, Proceedings*
Shri N. N. Yaji, Travel Arrangements and Reception***
Mrs. Chandrika Guttal, Chairman; Mrs. Mira Mahadevan, Mrs. Purbi Pandey, and Shri B. D. Tiwari, Registration and Reception
Shri R. Parthasarathi and Shri R. Achuthan, Program Arrangements**

APPENDIX B

The World Conference for International Peace Through Religion

IN DECEMBER 1924, the Church Peace Union meeting in New York City discussed "a plan to hold a World Religious Con-

---

* Permanent Staff, Gandhi Peace Foundation, 223 Rouse Avenue, New Delhi 1, India.

** Permanent Staff, Gandhi Centenary Committee, Rajghat, New Delhi 1, India.

*** Permanent Staff, Gandhi Memorial Trust, Rajghat, New Delhi 1, India.

**** Director, Promotion and Public Relations, The Methodist Church, Washington Area, 100 Maryland Avenue, N.E., Washington, D.C., 20002, U.S.A. Christian (Methodist).

***** Director, Publicity, Unitarian Universalist Association, 25 Beacon Street, Boston, Massachusetts, 02108, U.S.A. Unitarian Universalist.

gress in behalf of International Friendship and Goodwill."
The outline contemplated an international committee of 1,000
individuals. It was hoped to hold the Congress no later than
1930, but several suggested 1927. It was voted that the Church
Peace Union "accept responsibility" for calling the Congress.
The purpose was not to form a league of faiths, but to "har-
ness to the cause of international goodwill and peace the
spiritual force of all . . . religious faiths." Immediately a
group of American sponsors gave warm support to the plan,
including Jane Addams, Mrs. Franklin D. Roosevelt, Charles
E. Hughes, and Walter Lippmann.

Henry A. Atkinson, general secretary of the Church Peace
Union, was commissioned to survey the possibilities of a congress among the religions of the East. In September 1924,
a meeting with 191 delegates was held in Geneva to begin the
planning. Of these, 125 were Christians and thirteen Bahaists.
It was decided to call the world conference "in 1930 if
possible." It was agreed that the sole purpose of the conference would be "to rouse and to direct the religious impulses
of humanity against war in a constructive worldwide effort to
achieve peace."

The specific objectives of the conference were listed: 1. To
state the highest teachings of each religion on peace and the
causes of war. 2. To record the efforts of religious bodies in
furtherance of peace. 3. To devise means by which men of all
religious faiths may work together to remove existing obstacles to peace. 4. To seek opportunities for concerted action
among the adherents of all religions against the spirit of
violence.

A central executive committee of seventy persons was
formed. Six sections were set up—in Frankfurt, Paris, New
York, London, Athens, Peking, Tokyo, and Jerusalem. The
executive committee met in August 1929, in Frankfurt. Dr.
Atkinson reported that, in visiting India, China, and Japan,

he had interviewed Gandhi and Tagore. An All-India Committee had been set up, representative of "every religion and every class in India." Similar bodies were constituted in Burma and Ceylon. Dr. Atkinson met officials of the Japanese Government Department of Religions and they appointed an official committee to cooperate in preparing for the conference.

Dr. Atkinson generally concluded that "the proposal to hold the World Conference is timely; it gains a response from every group and every individual to whom it is presented." He added that "a great deal of intensive promotional work needs to be done in China, for no matter how completely the religions of the world may be represented, unless there is strong representation from China, the most important country at present in its influence for peace or war, the rest of the world will be neglected."

The Frankfurt meeting realized the complexity of organizing a conference and set up four international commissions of investigation: 1. To survey the influences in the world that make for war. 2. To inventory the spiritual resources of mankind with which these influences can be met. 3. To survey the efforts made by the various religions, religious agencies, and their adherents to further peace. 4. To enumerate methods by which these resources may be set in motion, coordinated, and directed to bear upon the causes of war. In addition, it was suggested that auxiliary commissions be set up by Japan, China, India, and other countries. The name of the meeting was officially changed from the Universal Religious Peace Conference to the World Conference for International Peace through Religion and the date postponed to 1931.

During the period the Japan Religious Association simultaneously conceived the idea of convening a World Religious Peace Conference. When the Japanese group heard of the

American plans, it postponed its own plans and decided to cooperate with the Church Peace Union. The Japanese Association decided, however, to hold a National Religious Conference as part of the enthronement ceremonies for the new emperor. This was held in June 1928, with 1,500 participants from the various Japanese religions.

To help organize Japanese preparation in the world conference, the Japan National Committee for a World Conference for International Peace Through Religion was formed in April 1930, by the Japan Religious Association and other groups. Fifty-eight persons were put on the committee, representing Buddhism, Shintoism, Confucianism, and Christianity. Rev. Shinichiro Imaoka (who helped guide the American Exploratory Mission around Tokyo in 1967) proposed that a National Religious Conference for International Peace be held in Japan. This was held in May 1931, with 345 delegates. After the opening ceremonies, including congratulatory addresses by the prime minister and the leaders of three faiths, and of the League of Nations Association, there were four lectures on Shinto, Buddhist, Christian, and Confucian teachings regarding peace. On the second day there were sectional meetings on religion and ethics, general culture, and practical problems. On the third day the conference held a general meeting at which twelve resolutions were unanimously adopted.

The major resolution of the Conference in part stated:

> If all religionists in the world cooperate and do their utmost, then our ideal of a warless world will not only exist in our religious faith, but also it will become a matter of practical international affairs. Therefore, we appeal to public opinion at home and abroad, proclaiming our belief and decision:
>   1. The Conference declares that we religionists should assume responsibility for the frequent occurrence of war.

2. The Conference declares that all religions can and ought to cooperate to bring about international peace, admitting the unique characteristics of each religion.

3. It is our conviction that the moral law should govern international relations as well as personal relations. . . .

7. The Conference hopes for the total removal of all racial and religious discrimination.

8. The Conference declares that religionists should take the leadership of the League of Nations and the Treaty for Renunciation of War to facilitate their ends . . .

There was a resolution relating to disarmament questions, indicating that it was "most gratifying to realize that in February 1932, there will be held the General Conference for Reduction and Limitation of Armaments . . ." Finally, there were resolutions urging the establishment of an institute for studying the means and ways of promoting international peace through cooperation of all religions and urging the creation of a permanent religious peace movement to make a world league of religions and pledging Japan's leadership in that kind of movement.

The executive committee for the World Conference next met in Berne in August 1930. The date for the conference was further postponed to 1932 with Washington as the venue. The committee pointed to "a world-wide movement rather than the holding of a single meeting." Albert Einstein in Berlin and Rabindranath Tagore in Calcutta agreed to be members of commissions. Meeting in Geneva in August 1931, the executive committee was told by its chairman, Dean Mathews of Chicago, that they were engaged in "an adventure" which had no precedents. The reports from some of the commissions which met called for national preparatory committees. As the preparations enlarged, the actual convening of the conference seemed to recede. The next meeting was held in September 1937. Because of increased international economic depression in the early thirties and the increased international tensions in the late thirties, it was apparent that the conference would be deferred. The preparatory committee asked that the conference be an agenda item of the 1938 meeting of the World Alliance for International Friendship Through the Churches.

The final report of the executive committee of the conference asserted that "the World Conference for International Peace through Religion holds the key that will unlock and open the door that leads to life fuller and greater than has ever hitherto been possible and that will cause the nations no longer to pass through the door, now open so wide, leading to destruction and to death." The final question was asked: "Will the Conference use that key and thus open the door of life without a moment's delay and so preserve the people of all nations from the dreadful fate which now threatens them?" In adjourning, the executive committee voted that a conference be held "at the earliest practicable date." It listed its assets: 1. New connections between men of goodwill among the religions of the East and West. 2. A fund of experience and information, the want of which in the earlier years retarded its efforts. 3. The organization of forces will be ready when the moment comes. The moment did not come; instead World War II began.

BIBLIOGRAPHY

MacFarland, Charles S. *Pioneers for Peace Through Religion.* New York: H. Revell Co. 1946.

The Japan National Conference for International Peace Through Religion. Tokyo. 1931.

Contributors to This Volume

Dr. Ralph David Abernathy is vice-president and treasurer of the Southern Christian Leadership Conference in the U.S.A. (He was a close associate of the late Dr. Martin Luther King, Jr., and has since been named president of the SCLC, succeeding Dr. King.)

Dr. Bool Chand is director of the Ahiṁsā Shodh-Peeth in New Delhi.

Rt. Rev. John H. Burt is bishop coadjutor of Ohio, U.S.A.

Shri U. N. Dhebar is chairman of the Khadi Board and former president of the Indian National Congress.

Hon. Morarji Desai is deputy prime minister of the government of India.

Shri R. R. Diwakar, M.P., is chairman of the Gandhi Peace Foundation.

Rabbi Maurice N. Eisendrath is president of the Union of American Hebrew Congregations. He is cochairman of the U.S. Inter-Religious Committee on Peace.

Archbishop Angelo Fernandes is secretary of the Catholic Bishops' Conference in India.

Rev. G. Nichidatsu Fujii is president of the Japanese-Indian Sarvodaya Friendship Association. He is a former co-worker with Mahatma Gandhi.

Jambel D. Gomboev, Bandido Hambo Lama, is chairman of the Religious Board of the Buddhists of the U.S.S.R.

Dr. Dana McLean Greeley is president of the Unitarian Universalist Association (of the United States and Canada). He is cochairman of the U.S. Inter-Religious Committee on Peace.

Rev. Herschel Halbert is secretary for International Affairs of the Episcopal Church, U.S.A. He is a member of the Secretariat of the U.S. Inter-Religious Committee on Peace.

Dr. Zakir Husain is President of India.

Dr. Homer A. Jack is director of the Division of Social Responsibility of the Unitarian Universalist Association (of the United States and Canada). He was joint secretary of the Symposium. He is also a member of the Secretariat of the U.S. Inter-Religious Committee on Peace.

Jagadguru Shri Gangadhar Rajayogeendra Mahaswamiji Moorusavirmath, Hubli, is a prominent Hindu leader.

Bishop John Wesley Lord is bishop of the Methodist Church, Washington Area, U.S.A. He is cochairman of the U.S. Inter-Religious Committee on Peace.

Dastoor N. D. Minochehr-Homji is a Parsi leader in Bombay, India.

Msgr. Edward G. Murray is pastor of the Sacred Heart Rectory in Roslindale, Massachusetts, U.S.A. He is secretary-treasurer of the U.S. Inter-Religious Committee on Peace.

Rev. Riri Nakayama is chief priest of the Hozenji Buddhist temple in Tokyo, Japan.

Shri Jayaprakash Narayan is a prominent Sarvodaya worker in India.

Shri G. Ramachandran, M.P., is chairman of the Subcommittee for International Seminars of the National Committee for the Gandhi Centenary in India and secretary of the Gandhi Peace Foundation. He was joint secretary of the Symposium.

Swami Ranganathananda is head of the Ramakrishna Mission Institute of Culture in Calcutta, India.

Prof. K. G. Saiyadain is with the Asian Institute of Educational Planning and Administration in New Delhi, India.

Dr. Gopal Singh, M.P., is the author of several works on Sikhism.

Dr. Karan Singh is minister of tourism in the government of India.

Hon. Harold E. Stassen is an attorney and layman in the Baptist church in the U.S.A.

Ven. Baddeeama Wimalawansa Thero is principal of the Shri Lawka Vidyalaya in Colombo, Ceylon.